"In a simple and heartfelt manner, Pat Gohn breaks open the meaning of being a woman, offering insights and encouragement from her own experience. In a world filled with messages distorting the real beauty of womanhood, *Blessed, Beautiful, and Bodacious* is a breath of fresh air. Inspirational, yet very practical!"

Anastasia Northrup
President of Theology of the Body International Alliance

"How desperately humanity needs to reclaim the true beauty and dignity of woman, for as woman goes, so goes the human race. Pat Gohn's book is a great gift in this regard. She demonstrates that the Catholic Church's true vision of woman is, indeed, bold and audacious—*bodacious!*"

Christopher West
Author of *At the Heart of the Gospel*

"Pat Gohn's new book is exactly what the title suggests. It is 'blessed' in that it takes joy in the best Christian thinking on the dignity of women available today. It is 'beautiful' in that it offers a personal reflection of one soul coming to know Jesus perhaps in the best way one can do that, through devotion to his holy Mother. And it is 'bodacious' in its recommendation that, despite feminism and all its works, Mary remains the 'still point of the turning world,' the model for every woman, especially modern women.

While focusing on women and their peculiar gifts—receptivity, generosity, sensitivity, and maternity— the book rises to a delightful and inspiring vision of every Catholic's mission to evangelize in Jesus' name."

Janet Benestad
Secretary for Faith Formation and Evangelization
Archdiocese of Boston

"When Pope John Paul II coined the phrase 'feminine genius,' women everywhere rejoiced. And then we asked ourselves, 'Um, what is it?' Women have been through so many vicissitudes in the twentieth century and into the twenty-first century that we are often a little unsure about who we are and what makes us great. We can even be quite out of touch with God's amazing design and plan for us—body and soul. *Blessed, Beautiful and Bodacious* will not only get you in touch with your true nature as a woman and give you permission to celebrate it, but it might even give you permission to let some things you don't need go."

Sr. Helena Burns, F.S.P.
Author of *He Speaks to You*

"Beautifully written and wonderfully insightful, this book is a joy and an inspiration. Pat Gohn is creative, courageous, and profound in her writing. She skillfully weaves Catholic teaching with genuine human experience. Every Catholic woman (and many men) will benefit from reading this book."

Rev. Dave Dwyer, C.S.P.
Host of *The Busted Halo Show*

"Gohn is the trusted friend with whom you wish to sit and enjoy a cup of coffee and a conversation. She's the 'bodacious' gal who will have you laughing out loud and noting the great joy to be found in everyday blessings in life. She's the profound catechist who will hold your hand and draw you closer to Christ. Live, love, and laugh with Gohn and you'll soon discover that you too are blessed, beautiful, and yes, even bodacious in your own unique way!"

Lisa M. Hendey
Author of *A Book of Saints for Catholic Moms*

"Forty years after the message that 'women can do and be anything' began to really resonate and take root within the culture, many women feel like they have the 'doing' part down pretty well, but they're not sure about the 'being.' What does it mean to 'be' and where can we find a consistent narrative of being that is of a piece with the realities of women's daily lives? Through her sometimes deeply personal stories and an insightful use of resources, Pat Gohn makes a convincing argument that—contrary to most media messaging—the Catholic Church has been sharing a view of the fullness of feminine genius, strength, and beauty that is downright holistic at its well-rounded depths. *Blessed, Beautiful, and Bodacious* is such a perfectly-timed (and sanely, gently offered) look at the 'being' part of modern womanhood that I cannot help but think the Holy Spirit wants this message out!"

Elizabeth Scalia
Author of *Strange Gods*

"In *Blessed, Beautiful, and Bodacious*, Pat Gohn joyfully and humorously leads the reader through candid anecdotes that illustrate the different facets and incredible depth of womanhood. This is a great read for women of all walks of life who desire to live to the full their vocations in modern world."

Rev. Michael Gaitley, M.I.C.
Director of the Association of Marian Helpers

Blessed, Beautiful, and Bodacious

Celebrating the Gift of Catholic Womanhood

To Sheila!
you are God's
beloved daughter! Pat Gohn

Pat Gohn

Foreword by Terry Polakovic,
Executive Director of Endow

AVE MARIA PRESS **AVE** Notre Dame, Indiana

© 2012 by Patricia W. Gohn

All rights reserved. No part of this book may be used or reproduced in any manner whatsoever, except in the case of reprints in the context of reviews, without written permission from Ave Maria Press®, Inc., P.O. Box 428, Notre Dame, IN 46556.

Founded in 1865, Ave Maria Press is a ministry of the United States Province of Holy Cross.

www.avemariapress.com

Paperback: ISBN-10 1-59471-370-7, ISBN-13 978-1-59471-370-5

E-book: ISBN-10 1-59471-371-5, ISBN-13 978-1-59471-371-2

Cover images © Thinkstock Images.

Cover and text design by Katherine Robinson Coleman.

Printed and bound in the United States of America.

Library of Congress Cataloging-in-Publication Data

Gohn, Pat.
  Blessed, beautiful, and bodacious : celebrating the gift of Catholic womanhood / by Pat Gohn ; foreword by Terry Polakovic.
    p. cm.
  ISBN 978-1-59471-370-5 (pbk.) -- ISBN 1-59471-370-7 (pbk.)
  1. Women--Religious aspects--Catholic Church. 2. Catholic women--Religious life. I. Title.
  BX2347.8.W6G64 2013
  248.8'43--dc23
                          2012039831

To Jesus through Mary.

With deep gratitude to she who is

blessed among women—

Momma Mary—

for her tender patience

with my learning curve.

Thank you, *women who are mothers!* You have sheltered human beings within yourselves in a unique experience of joy and travail. This experience makes you become God's own smile upon the newborn child, the one who guides your child's first steps, who helps it to grow, and who is the anchor as the child makes its way along the journey of life.

Thank you, *women who are wives!* You irrevocably join your future to that of your husbands, in a relationship of mutual giving, at the service of love and life.

Thank you, *women who are daughters* and *women who are sisters!* Into the heart of the family, and then of all society, you bring the richness of your sensitivity, your intuitiveness, your generosity and fidelity.

Thank you, *women who work!* You are present and active in every area of life-social, economic, cultural, artistic and political. In this way you make an indispensable contribution to the growth of a culture which unites reason and feeling, to a model of life ever open to the sense of "mystery", to the establishment of economic and political structures ever more worthy of humanity.

Thank you, *consecrated women!* Following the example of the greatest of women, the Mother of Jesus Christ, the Incarnate Word, you open yourselves with obedience and fidelity to the gift of God's love. You help the Church and all mankind to experience a "spousal" relationship to God, one which magnificently expresses the fellowship which God wishes to establish with his creatures.

Thank you, *every woman*, for the simple fact of being *a woman!* Through the insight which is so much a part of your womanhood you enrich the world's understanding and help to make human relations more honest and authentic.

John Paul II, *Letter to Women*, 1995, 2

Contents

Foreword

Pat Gohn might call it bodacious.

I guess it was.

It was that moment ten years ago when I was about to do the thing that would change everything. I was walking toward Archbishop Charles J. Chaput's office in the Denver chancery with butterflies in my stomach and a lump in my throat. Would he accept the proposal I was about to audaciously lob across his desk? Was I bold enough to do it?

What I had was an idea—an idea for a women's apostolate that had taken hold of me and would not let go. Together with a small band of Catholic friends, I had become enthralled by the writings of John Paul II, especially *Mulieris Dignitatem*, *Letter to Women*, and the many teachings collectively known as theology of the body. What was so attractive about these writings? Simply this: they celebrated the gift of womanhood!

Women are lovingly made in God's image and likeness, and knowing this—really knowing it in the depths of our being—inspires us to be the women he created us to be. John Paul II called woman's unique, irreplaceable quality her "feminine genius."

I was convinced "Endow" was an idea whose time had come. It was a dream of sharing these truths with Catholic women by creating an educational program that would not just excite them—but ignite them—to trust and live the beauty and truth of the faith. We were sure that women understanding the truth of *who* they are and *whose* they are could change the world!

Could I convince the archbishop?

Indeed, Archbishop Chaput "read the signs of the times" as Vatican II calls us to do, and he saw the potential for good in such a ministry, even beyond what I could see myself. Thus, Endow started the journey of becoming what it is today—a women's ministry nearly 20,000 souls strong, preaching the truth of God's love and the genius of women.

In these pages, Pat Gohn seeks to do the same thing by sharing her life experiences and the Church's teaching that women are indeed blessed, beautiful, and bodacious. Like me, Pat is among the ranks of women who have fallen in love with the Church's teaching on the gift of our womanhood and have been changed and challenged by it. Long a favorite with people who follow her podcasts and read her columns, she has a particular wisdom and a delightful way of sharing it with the women who need it most.

As Endow's cofounder and executive director, I'm happy to say that *Blessed, Beautiful, and Bodacious* and Endow are of one mind. Pat and I both seek to communicate that when women appreciate and nurture their "feminine genius" through prayer and faith-filled living, they are equipped to do the urgent work of transforming the culture into a civilization of love.

Pat might describe my action ten years ago as a bodacious—bold and audacious—move, stepping out in faith to pursue a dream that I was sure the Holy Spirit had planted in my heart. The book you hold in your hands will challenge you to imagine the effect when you embrace your vocation to live your true calling as a woman made in God's image.

And here's something else to hold on to: there is something wonderful God needs from you and only you. Find that thing that is yours alone. Whatever your dream, let the Holy

Spirit be your guide and your inspiration. You are blessed. You are beautiful. Be bodacious!

Terry Polakovic
Endow* Cofounder and Executive Director
September 8, 2012
Feast of the Nativity of the Blessed Virgin Mary

*Learn more about this exciting ministry at
www.endowgroups.org

Introduction

You Had Me at *Bodacious!*

So what are we to make of these words describing women as *blessed, beautiful,* and *bodacious?*

It's the name of an all-woman singing group I would have formed if I were to sing this book to you. That or Triple-B, but that name might be confused with my other rock band where I play rhythm guitar: Babes, Bibles, and Benedict.

Kidding! Really. Just kidding.

I don't know where your mind just went, but mine went to cute, irresistible Gerber babies; the Bible apps on my iPhone; and at the time of this writing, the coolest octogenarian on the planet, Pope Benedict XVI. All of this might identify me as a middle-aged woman who misses holding babies every day and looks forward to grandchildren, a believer with geeky new media habits, and well, a Catholic who thinks you should just get better and, sweeter with age.

Back to the book title: *Blessed, Beautiful, and Bodacious.*

Blessed evokes something of the sacred and the higher things. A woman needs to know she is blessed, that she is a treasure, and the reasons why. This blessing is derived from the sources of a woman's dignity.

Beautiful . . . I've yet to meet a woman not seeking to be beautiful in some sense of the word. When it comes to the gifts of femininity, every woman has them. No woman was left out when God handed out these beauties. Let's hear what makes them sing.

Bodacious is a bit bolder than the first two words, depending on your point of view. For me, *bodacious* is a compliment meaning "remarkable" or "most excellent." It sounds one

1

part attractive and one part audacious, both descriptors of many women, too. I offer *bodacious* in a spirit of good will and respect for the extraordinary mission women are called to live.

Blessed, Beautiful, and Bodacious seeks to celebrate womanhood by exploring a woman's dignity, gifts, and mission. The three parts of this book contain introductory conversations on these themes, not the final word on them. I'm a gal you might find next to you in the pew just as easily as you'd find me pouring coffee for a friend. I relish those moments when someone leans in, saying, "I really love this, and I'd love to share it." That's what church and coffee and friends are for. And that's why I write.

My research for this book has been tested in the school of life even though my training and work classifies me a certifiable theology book nerd. If you like what you read here, there are many authors who can you take you much deeper. I suggest further readings and resources for each of these topics at the end of the book.

I've long volunteered in and been employed by Catholic parishes. Conversations with women over the years tell me we need to hear more about women's topics in church. My favorite conversations are with women yearning to go deeper with God and in their mission in life, whether in their families or in their work.

Yet when I speak to women in faith settings, it is not uncommon for me to find a woman who cannot articulate what makes her special in the eyes of God, the Church, or the world. Meanwhile the Catholic Church has been proclaiming a rich, empowering message to women for years. Sadly, not every woman has heard it. I know, I was one of them.

So, I started taking notes on what I found meaningful for me as a woman. Then I began sharing my findings with women in churches and on websites through my columns and my podcast, *Among Women*. And here we are.

Blessed, Beautiful, and Bodacious is what I've learned about womanhood from God, the Bible, the teachings of the Church, and from people who've loved me along the way. Much more than giving me a few new adjectives to express my joy in being a woman, as this book's title suggests, coming to know the gift of my womanhood has brought me into a deeper relationship with God, my husband, family, and countless others, including—much to my surprise—Mary. That's Mary, as in the Blessed Virgin Mary, the Mother of Jesus, whom you'll find I've spent a lot of time avoiding. If Mary had played guitar on stage in the seventies I might have thought she was cooler sooner. Back then, if you wanted to get my attention, you had better be carrying a six-string.

When I was a young girl, I dreamed about playing the guitar.

I trace my love for music to childhood memories of spinning 45rpm records on my parents' portable phonograph. In pre-adolescence I spent hours listening to the stereo, an RCA Magnavox. Back then stereo consoles were pieces of furniture housing an automatic stackable turntable, an AM/FM radio, and a cabinet to store a record collection. I dusted the thing for years during my Saturday chores. Most of all, I loved playing deejay and cueing up the records.

My parents owned an album by Chet Atkins, a big-time Grammy winner who was nicknamed "Mister Guitar." His sound is synonymous with Gretsch electric guitars.

It was love at first chord. The joy and the life that came from that guitar captivated me. Thanks to Chet, I set my mind on playing guitar someday. I was nine. I didn't know any of the music basics. Yet.

So I prayed desperate prayers to God, like little Catholic schoolgirls are wont to do, for a seemingly impossible dream

. . . a guitar. There was the usual dropping of big hints to my parents in hope of such a miracle. Meanwhile I became a radio junkie, listening to all the pop stations beaming out of New York City on my Emerson radio. Slowly my musical tastes veered beyond the family album collection to mainstream pop such as the Beatles, the Beach Boys, and the iconic folk-rockers of the seventies.

One Christmas, I received the blessing I had longed for. My parents bought me a beginner's acoustic guitar. I had no idea how much that gift would eventually bless me, but I just knew it was the greatest gift I had ever received. Weeks later, I began lessons with a hip mustachioed musician in a colorful sports jacket. Imagine my swoon at that first lesson when I saw that my instructor played a gleaming electric guitar like Chet's!

The most meaningful gifts are the ones that come from someone who loves you, the ones that offer a promise of something more than the gift itself, the ones that say "I believe in you." And so, with the promise of lessons being an investment in my future, the good things to come were an even greater blessing.

That guitar and those lessons played a powerful role in my becoming the woman I am today. Learning to play music opened me up to a whole new way of relating to the world. It made me unique in my family; no one else played an instrument. Once I mastered the basics, I jumped at chances to play with others. Soon that guitar was part of my identity.

Music introduced me to new friends. In my class, I bonded over music with girls who were guitarists too. Musical camaraderie staved off some of the awkwardness of puberty, when many girls start getting clique-ish.

I was in a Girl Scout troop at the local public school. Being from a Catholic school made me a bit of an outsider, but music at scout camp and troop events helped me make friends. Music has a way of building community where none exists. Through scouts I began singing, and my confidence grew. Soon, my deep baritone was noticed at school when we sang at Mass. The nun in charge of liturgical music often asked me to lead the boys singing parts, so she could lead the girls. I learned to harmonize out of necessity.

Music helped my faith grow, and it strengthened my bond to the Church. In some ways, I think I loved music before I really loved God. Singing and playing at church became very special to me. It gave me a sense of belonging and freedom to express myself. Through singing I learned what it means to pray with the heart, not just by rote.

Music made me beautiful. When you are fourteen, you need things that remind you of that.

On the inside, music created a connection with God in the sanctuary of my heart. It also helped me connect on an emotional level with people. Music became a bridge toward getting to know people and being approachable; it was one of the first ways I began to share my faith with others. Between the prayer and the community it brought, music was a gift that kept on giving. I always liked creative writing in school, so it wasn't long before I wrote songs for church and friends.

Music softened me on the outside, too. I had always been a bit of a tomboy, somewhat loud, competitive, and sort of rough and gritty for a girl, much to the consternation of my very ladylike mother. My clothes were perpetually sporting grass stains. Still, music helped me discover my emerging feminine side—the part of me that noticed a boy might be more than someone to outrace on my bike and the part that listened to love songs and wondered what it would be like to fall for someone like that. I attended school dances with the boys I knew, but the music always captivated me more than the dancing.

I didn't realize it until much later, but popular music introduced me to the ideals of feminism, too. Helen Reddy's "I Am Woman" would play on the Emerson at night, as the beat of female empowerment permeated the Top 40.

My first taste of being a girl who broke into an all-boys club was my brief stint in a garage band playing rhythm guitar with three boys who adored the Stones and Led Zeppelin. I don't know who was impressed more—the girls who saw what I was doing or the boys who were amazed that I could play. I did not yet have the maturity to discern that my playing "Sympathy for the Devil" was no "Stairway to Heaven." I was just happy to be strumming along as we competed in a battle of the bands to play for future school dances.

Sooner or later, jamming with musicians from school, scouts, and church began to pay off. I was getting paid for musical accompaniment at weddings and elsewhere. Youth ministry was springing up in my parish, and yours truly was always providing music for the retreats and meetings.

God started to get my attention, too. On a retreat, I committed my heart to Jesus Christ and never looked back. That commitment led me slowly to reprioritize things in my life. Sometime after that conversion moment, I realized God was inviting me to use my guitar playing and writing gifts for his purposes.

You could say that my guitar playing led me to my vocation and avocations. This gift blessed me and shaped me in beautiful ways. It was like God was orchestrating it, and that was the most bodacious thing of all to discover: God really did have a plan and a purpose for my life.

Music introduced me to the love of my life, my future husband, Bob. No surprise! He was a talented guitar player I had met in high school. Guess what? He played all those fancy jazz chords and arpeggios—just like Chet! Bob played in a band, too. Eventually he joined me playing at church weddings. Funny that years later, we had a wedding of our own!

My love of music and writing fostered my interest in radio, and I pursued a communications degree. I worked as an on-air deejay and as a copywriter in radio for several years. None of that would have been possible without my interest, knowledge, acceptance, and application of the basics—the musical basics.

Mastering the basics of music was a small price to pay for all the joy it brought me. Most of all, applying what I learned changed my life, opening a new world of relationships and experiences. A lot of life is like that. But first we've got to know what the basics are to unlock their potential for our growth.

The same holds in the Christian life. When the basics are in order—love of God followed by love of neighbor—we're well on our way to responding in love to all the relationships and experiences we have in life.

For a woman's life, discovering the basics might begin by asking questions like "Who am I?" and "What are my gifts?" and "What's my purpose in life?"

Why bother talking about these things at all?

Simple.

Women are blessed, beautiful, and bodacious. Too many women doubt that about themselves.

What's more, Christianity values and esteems womanhood much more than our present culture does. Some women are not sure what to make of that. I mean, that might sound kind of old school to a modern woman. Yet I've found that the Catholic Church has been singing the praises of women out loud and has a view of femininity that is blessed, beautiful, and yes, downright bodacious. Pope John Paul II lauded it as the "feminine genius" (*Mulieris Dignitatem* [Apostolic Letter on the Dignity and Vocation of Women], 30, 31).

Still, a lot of women might doubt that the Church has a good opinion of them.

Over time, I've accepted being blessed and beautiful, though the meaning of those words has changed from my youthful definitions.

What has impressed me about my own faith experience is that I'm always coming across new things that bless me and help me to grow. The Catholic faith traces its roots back centuries, and still I find new things that pique my interest and have direct application to my life. It's attractive, enduring wisdom. I find that a great comfort, an anchor steadying me against twisting tides (Heb 6:19), a perennial song that runs through the soundtrack of my life.

Within this old and wise faith, there is also a new brand of feminism afoot, attracting women with its smart, empowering message and a new evangelization, or a retelling of the familiar Christian story with a new passion.

But none of this is worth discussing unless we get to the basics. What are the notes in the chords of this new melody?

What are the things that make women blessed, beautiful, and bodacious?

Our dignity, gifts, and mission.

Blessed? All persons are created with a sublime dignity they did not earn. By calling you into existence and creating you, God did something unique. He fashioned a one-of-a-kind woman. She has never existed before, yet she will exist into eternity. If you've ever admired a masterpiece of art or music, you understand an original work of genius.

The baptized Christian has an added blessing. God's care and power are invoked, and a woman enters God's family. God will never divorce, disown, or unfriend us. We belong. We are beloved. This is a God who is singing a love song over us. (See Zep 3:17.)

Our dignity arrives at the moment of our conception and in the moment of our Baptism. It's about *who* we are and *whose* we are.

A woman's dignity is a blessing. The sacred character of this blessing is derived from God's plan for a woman. Her core identities flow from her being created by God as a feminine human person and her Baptism that graces her as a beloved daughter of God and a member of the Body of Christ, the Church. The blessing is akin to light, an inner spark that flows from God to a woman's core. It lights her from within, allowing her to be a radiant light-bearer to others.

Beautiful? Okay. I've heard all the complaints women have—even from some of the most gorgeous women I know.

"Sure, God just might have something to say about my being blessed and all, but have you seen me? Beautiful? Are you kidding?"

"You know, there's a lot of competition among the ladies out there. The media images of beauty are too far out of reach."

Few women I know really understand the depth of their own beauty because they are too busy comparing themselves with others or have been unfairly compared—and rejected—by others. I get that. I've dealt with my own body issues and flaws. One priest advises, "Compare and despair!"

Most issues about beauty or body originate from unrealistic standards and pressures in today's culture. What's worse, fashion and vogue are always changing.

But what if I told you that there is a level playing field? What if you found out that every woman has gifts that make her beautiful—beauty derived from something innate and eternal and not fleeting or skin-deep? These gifts sing in sync with the beauty of a woman's inborn femininity, a standard for true beauty far beyond mere appearances.

Women are uniquely endowed with gifts of receptivity, generosity, sensitivity, and maternity. When we trust these things, we become beautiful from the inside out. We live the lives we are born to live, becoming the best women we can be. When we exercise our gifts, beauty always emerges.

Receptivity is tied to a woman's nature. It is openness to others characterized by a *yes* that actively responds to the people and the world. Receptivity draws people in and celebrates their presence.

Generosity gives freely. It relinquishes the what's-mine-versus-what's-yours mentality. Women who practice generosity are passionate lovers of their true spouses. They have learned how to make a sincere gift of self to their beloved.

Women who excel in sensitivity have x-ray vision of the hearts around them. Okay. Maybe that's an exaggeration. But a sensitive woman sees others with her heart. She is a visionary seeing into situations that require a delicate touch.

Finally, there is the gift of maternity, being a life-bearer to others through motherhood. We've all known maternal nurturers. Not all of them were biological mothers. A woman's selfless mothering love and service can be life-giving in physical and spiritual ways.

I describe these four qualities of femininity as gifts for two reasons: they are beautiful gifts to women from God, and they are beautiful gifts from women to others, enabling women to be bearers of love to the world.

Bodacious? A young woman I know told me she loved the title of this book, saying, "You had me at *bodacious!*" It's a word I love, too. But I don't suggest flipping to those chapters first since the *blessed* and the *beautiful* really do lay the two rails of track for the *bodacious* train to travel upon.

The most excellent women, the bodacious women, are women who authentically live their dignity and gifts. They don't keep beauty and blessing to themselves. They lovingly lavish it upon others. They are capable and wise, or they are seeking to grow in that direction. Their love is spoken and unspoken. It wells up rather naturally in them, and their ability to stretch and serve sends positive ripple effects into the world.

Bodaciousness is maternity magnified. Bodacious women are those whose lives have the most purpose and meaning when they give their love away and when their love takes shape in others. These are the women who embody physical or spiritual motherhood. Often they embody both. They live and lead from a place of empowering love.

The bodacious mission of a woman's life allows her beauty and blessing to work in tandem. It's a calling to deeply love, from a source rooted in the universal dignity and gifts of her person. That being said, the mission of a woman's life is also specific and unique to her talents and circumstances. Both the universal and unique call on a woman's life challenge her to be a source of truth, beauty, and goodness in the world.

Physical and spiritual motherhood is characterized by a bodacious fullness, an all-in willingness to lay one's life down for the sake of another in small and large ways. Bodacious women live their mission in sync with the mission of the Church by making disciples in both physical and spiritual ways, bearing new life in the world. They are women who give birth to families by bearing children. They are women who give birth to communities and good works in others by bearing the good news.

One woman who lives these ideas heroically and, dare I say, bodaciously is the Blessed Virgin Mary. We'll be looking to her for inspiration as we explore the basics of our dignity, gifts, and mission.

When it comes to Mary, I think there are two groups of believers. The first group contains the people who fall in love with Jesus first. After a while, Jesus smiles and says, "Wait till you meet my mother!" (You'd expect that kind of behavior from a gentleman. You know that the relationship with Jesus is getting serious when he brings his mother into the picture!) The second group usually includes Catholics who have met Mary in their spiritual journey, and they readily identify with her motherly love. One day she smiles and says, "Have I got someone special for you. You've got to meet my son!"

I'm in the first group. I thought I knew a lot about the love of God and neighbor, but I did not fully embrace my dignity, gifts, and mission as a woman until Jesus introduced me to his mother. To use a musical metaphor, Mary taught me to sing harmony. Having her in my life has made all the parts of my feminine life symphonic and more in tune.

Besides Mary, I've experienced the "feminine genius" in action in the many bodacious women who have mothered and mentored me.

More than anything since my initial conversion to Christ, nothing has opened me to living the fullness of my faith in and through my womanhood than discovering the basics of my dignity, gifts, and mission. Everything is better harmonized—faithful, joyful, and free.

There's been lasting impact.

Kind of like what happened to me when I picked up that guitar.

Part One

THE BLESSED

DIGNITY

OF WOMEN

I used to write radio commercials for a living, so I'm always interested when I find a commercial that has meaningful copy, like the priceless-themed commercials for MasterCard. If I were writing a commercial today, here's the one I'd create.

Picture this scene: A middle-aged woman is shopping in a high-end toy store, and we hear the announcer say, "Cost of a custom-made teddy bear? Fifty dollars." Next she is seated on a plane with the teddy bear on her lap. Again the announcer intones, "Cost of round-trip economy airfare? Four hundred dollars." In the final scene, the woman is delivering the teddy bear to the newborn baby and her momma in a hospital maternity ward. Cue the announcer. "Meeting your grandchild a few hours after she is born? Priceless."

We all want to be happy. We all want to be loved. We all want to know that there's something special and perhaps even sacred about us, but we often fail in our ability to articulate it or trust that it is true. For all its money talk, the credit-card scenario I've described points to something beyond the price tags of goods and services: the most important things in life aren't things. Truth resonates; it communicates simply. We intuitively get it. Deep down, we don't really need to explain it.

Let's start to talk a few truths that makes you *you* and me *me*—the intangibles that point out that we are blessed, the intangibles that money can't buy. The truth is you can't buy a blessing; it's free. And priceless.

Chapter 1

Living
from
the
Inside Out

I just didn't think much of it. The nagging pain. I'd get over it.
I felt it on the treadmill when I set the machine for "incline."
It zinged me again walking down steps. At first I thought it
was a muscle pull. I would probably be fine in a few days.
I wasn't.

My physician sent me for x-rays. The results revealed I
had a congenital deformity known as bilateral hip dysplasia,
a malformation of my hip joints, a slow deterioration since
birth. Orthopedic specialists determined I would eventually
need two hip replacements.

This deformity had affected me most of my adult life without my awareness of it. How did this go undiagnosed for so long? My symptoms were increasing, but the true cause was missed. Pain flares were always blamed on something else. The back and leg pain during my three pregnancies had been attributed to sciatica, when in actuality it was the misaligned hips. Another time, following a car accident, my physical therapist could never figure out why my stance kept changing in ways unrelated to my injuries.

Of course, this is much easier to see with the proper diagnosis.

But here's the important point: I never knew I suffered from a deformity—I thought everything was normal! I believed my bones were healthy even though there was ongoing erosion in my condition.

Pain gets our attention. Coming into my forties, I was faced with chronic pain that made me limp. I kept a cane handy for long walks. I wore flats all the time and was able to put off surgery for quite a while. Eventually my deformed bone caused my right foot to turn inward. My leg muscles and knee ligaments atrophied to accommodate the new direction my hip took.

Pain increased and mobility decreased. I became downright grumpy for a year or more. Regrettably, I often treated the people that I loved poorly because I became so self-absorbed. One day I caught my scowling face in the mirror and did not recognize myself.

It was time. I made the appointment, signed the releases, and scheduled surgery to receive a new titanium hip joint.

The transformation in my physical and emotional health after surgery was nearly immediate. No longer was a deformity running and ruining my life with its pain. I found my smile again; the gal who got swallowed up in her own suffering was re-emerging. It was freeing on a physical and a spiritual level. Body and soul were breathing easier.

I had lived with this deformity for years without realizing the far-reaching impact. Something was wrong on the inside, and it affected everything on the outside, but I couldn't see it until pain got my attention. I had no idea about the new life that a correction would bring or how grateful I would be.

In the recovery period, I had to make adjustments. The new me needed to learn how to walk straight. The deformity in my hip was gone, but now the rest of me struggled to conform to its new direction. Leg muscles and ligaments stretched, causing their own new pains. There were some difficult moments in the rehab process, as I was adjusting to the new me. But with every step, I was getting stronger.

There are parallels here for our lives. Just as the bones give shape to the body from the inside out, so too the soul is the interior force—the spiritual principle—that animates each person. The body is the physical principle. Body and soul are beautifully joined, giving us each a unique shape and substance. This combination affords each of us an inherent dignity that is rooted in the fact that we are human. To further understand our dignity, we need to ponder the depths, the sacred unity of body and soul.

Our soul is that lovely intangible communicating the shape of our character, temperament, and personality. The soul—our interior—is expressed on the exterior through the body.

We often describe what delights us about the people we love by pointing out their sense of humor, creativity, sensitivity, strength, compassion, intellect, confidence, goodness, or honesty. What we're really describing is their interior attributes, the different aspects of their souls that stir us.

Yet we don't walk around saying we love someone's soul.
We name persons. We love Bob, Mom, or Mrs. Smith. We use
affectionate nicknames or terms of endearment to describe
the uniqueness of each individual.

The "soulishness" of a person, again, reveals that we live
from the inside out. Through words and actions, our bodies
reveal our very selves, the things that are soul-deep. Sometimes souls are hurting. We may suffer from identity "defor-
mities" that we've grown up with or something that we can't
really explain. Maybe we choose to ignore the aches for a
while, but they are harder to ignore over time. Hurt gets our
attention. Pain on the inside affects the way we walk. Putting
a good face on our pains gets us only so far.

Souls sometimes need healing much like bodies. Knowing
the Maker and Lover of our souls is as important as knowing
a good doctor. When spiritual principles are out of alignment
or malformed, we might not realize we are hurting ourselves
or others until it's too late. By then we are in pain or worse.
What we thought was normal was a "deformity." Meanwhile
the problem wearies us, yielding a kind of spiritual limp,
robbing us of strength and peace.

So let's try to deal with ourselves gently here, especially
if we think we might be limping spiritually. For the moment,
let's take a break and ponder the health of our soul.

One of the things that I love about my girlfriends is that
they always give me food for thought. I love to sit and chat
about life and consider the things that are on our minds. You
always know when we've crossed over into the real soul work
when, as we are sharing over a cup of coffee, our hearts spill
out across the table.

Good conversations always help me to ponder. They lead
me to wonder or consider things deeply. I weigh and sift
for truth. The subjects I spend the most time pondering are

usually the ones closest to my heart: love, relationships, faith, change, work, dreams, family, and the future.

Pondering happens on the inside. There's that living-from-the-inside-out again! If you and I were sitting at a coffee shop today, I'd invite you to ponder your interior self and how you live from the inside out. If you are limping, I'd encourage you to rest in these pages and consider God's good opinion of you. That's right. God thinks of you and loves you more than you know. Heck, God is crazy about you. But even if you cannot trust that right now, try suspending your judgment just for a little while—for the sake of having hope that you'll begin to understand God's good opinion of you as you read the coming chapters. Let's offer to ourselves a measure of self-respect and time to consider what's at the core of that claim.

Perhaps our ideas about ourselves have been formed by a cultural worldview that demeans us. Maybe a negative self-image comes from what other people have said or done to us. Perhaps we've done things that embarrass us. Maybe we've never dared to believe that we have any dignity at all.

I talk to many women in my work, and I've learned that some were never taught the important truths about our dignity or about the Christian faith. Maybe we've not been informed as to the incredible identity and destiny that we have. When we don't know the truth about ourselves, what fills the gap is often erroneous information, deforming our inner consciences. No one is immune from "stinkin' thinkin'" or the little movie scripts that play in our minds, chipping away at our dignity. Like the preset buttons on a car radio or the playlists we create on iTunes, repeated messages of the good songs can lift us up, but the negative ones can really bring us down. What's inside of us plays out in our daily lives, and it becomes problematic when we may have ways of thinking and acting that do not align with the goodness of our dignity.

Many of us cannot articulate what makes us special in the eyes of God, the Church, or the world. Or we harbor discontent about our life and purpose. Since we tend to live from the inside out, what's inside really matters.

Why? Our conscience is our most secret core and sanctuary. It is the part of us where we detect right and wrong; it is the core where we are challenged to do good things and avoid evil. In the conscience, we are alone with God. Sometimes the role of our conscience is referred to as the "quiet of our hearts," our "interior life," our "inner voice," or the "voice of truth."

When I was growing up, sometimes the decision-making voice of conscience was depicted in cartoons as a tiny angel perched on a shoulder and whispering into an ear. Meanwhile a tiny demon sat on the opposite shoulder yelling a negative message.

Here's an image that might prove meaningful for Catholic Christians: In Catholic churches, you'll find the tabernacle. A candle or a sanctuary light nearby reminds visitors that God's holy presence is within the tabernacle in the form of the consecrated bread of the Eucharist. In a certain sense, the conscience of your soul is also your tabernacle. It's at the heart of you. It's where the presence of God meets you in the person of who you are. St. Paul was the first to describe this concept: "Do you not know that your body is a temple of the Holy Spirit within you, which you have from God?" (1 Cor 6:19). If your body is a temple, then the conscience is like the holy of holies in the soul: the tabernacle. If you've been baptized, you have been consecrated like that holy bread in the tabernacle . . . you've been blessed.

Our soul's conscience is a sanctuary—a holy place, a sacred space that God designed so that he might dwell within us. It is the place of inner dialogue with God. It is the place of true prayer and the deepest pondering, meditation, and contemplation. Through the conscience, God will show us the truth about ourselves and about what we should do. It is the place where we come to understand what we believe about ourselves, others, and God. In turn, we will confront truth, beauty, and goodness; we will become aware of our blessings and blessedness. But for many of us, knowing that we are blessed might be hard to accept. We have too many distractions rattling our consciences and tempting us to discount our goodness.

The opinions of others find their way into our consciences because we bring our whole selves, including our memories, into this sanctuary. So our beliefs, what we've learned, and the things others have said or done to us also tend to fill our consciences.

Negative voices and emotional wounds can cause a noisy atmosphere in the quiet space of our consciences. Noise competes, impairing our ability to hear the voice of God and his truth. So we have to invite God in to fully occupy the tabernacle. If there is anyone or anything else we've invited to sit there with us, the noise will continue. If God does not reign in the tabernacle, someone or something else will.

Even now, we can turn to God and ask the Holy Spirit to come into us in a deeper way with a simple prayer: "Come, Holy Spirit." It may seem hard to ask if we've never done it before, but God's spirit is very adaptable. Just open the door a crack and invite him in. He can slip in and start doing some housecleaning. God wants to help us; as the Maker and Lover of our souls, he has a vested interest.

To be healthy, our conscience needs to be in tune with God and God's good opinion of us. The more we seek God's truth, the stronger and deeper our conscience will be and the less it will be blinded or dulled by a cheap substitute.

This strengthening and deepening suggests that a conscience is something that undergoes formation. It takes in and stores data. That is the reason the formation of a child's conscience is so important. What we believe about ourselves has relevance for daily life. It shapes our thinking and our emotional and spiritual well-being.

When God moves in our souls or consciences, it is like an inaudible yet alluring voice in our heart. God is the one true voice. If we pause long enough to listen, he calls us to ponder his truth.

When what we believe about ourselves is somehow broken, hurt, deformed, or damaged, the suffering we feel eventually cries out for healing, restoration, and transformation. What goes for bone structure holds for conscience formation. When what is inside is blessed and properly operational, when we are aligned with the way God designed us, we live more fruitful and happy lives. Call it cooperating with the beatitude of our blessedness.

A well-formed conscience embraces the blessing of *who* we are and *whose* we are. A good conscience is the key to how well we live and love. The more our conscience is aligned with what is true, good, and beautiful, the deeper our sense of being blessed will be. This is the blessing of being alive: we are designed, both in body and soul, to thrive not only in relationships with other people but also with God.

We must ponder this blessing.

But first, a few words about pondering and the woman I know who models that for us.

The Bible describes Mary, the mother of Jesus, as one who "ponders." She "keeps" things in her heart (Lk 1:29; 2:19, 51 NAB). She lives from the inside out. The Gospel of Luke references Mary's interior life three times. Mary's ponderings follow conversations she has had with Jesus or about him. They stir her heart and mind.

The first reference appears at the annunciation. The angel Gabriel greets Mary, hailing her as the favored one. She "was greatly troubled at what was said and *pondered* what sort of greeting this might be" (Lk 1:29 NAB; emphasis added). But God knows what is in Mary's heart, and immediately the angel announces the miraculous news that Mary has been chosen to be the mother of the Savior foretold in scripture.

The second time Luke references Mary's pondering follows the birth of Jesus. The shepherds arrive on the scene, relating the vision of the angelic choir appearing in the sky. After these dramatic conversations, Mary "kept all these things, *reflecting* on them in her heart" (Lk 2:19 NAB; emphasis added).

The third reference follows Mary's great relief in finding Jesus among the chief priests and elders of the Temple, after having feared he was missing. Mary conveys her concerns to Jesus who reminds her that all is well. He is busy doing his Father's work. Following this conversation, Mary "kept all these things in her heart" (Lk 2:51 NAB). And, I'm sure she brought them before God in the tabernacle of prayer.

I'd like to suggest Mary's method of pondering and reflecting as a way to consider the conversation we're having in this book. Ponder the implications of what you read and quietly examine your heart.

Pondering requires time and space. Pondering takes things to prayer. You'll know what's right because truth resonates and offers peace. Peace is the hallmark of the Holy

Spirit. It is one of the best indicators that you are following the dictates of a properly formed conscience.

Admittedly, I was slow to follow Mary's example in my life. Earlier, I did not trust her example. I'll share the roadblocks I've had, in case you've had some. So let's consider my early misgivings about Mary.

I mentioned how I came to know Jesus in my teens, and as I did, I read the Bible more and more. Of course, I came across Mary in the New Testament. Broadly speaking, I never discounted Mary's role in God's plan. I just never included her in any of mine. I kept a cordial distance and never openly disparaged her or the people devoted to her. I adopted a kind of live-and-let-live attitude toward her devotees.

Mary had little influence on me in my teens and twenties. Even though I had a Catholic upbringing, I have to say that the sociopolitical influences often held sway. The culture stressed a powerful feminism; it preached a woman's empowerment. I was schooled in the cultural cliché that told women that you are what you do. My generation was among the first expected to compete with men—not rely on them or trust them. "I am woman, hear me roar" was a common mantra. There was so much to achieve, and I was an eager achiever.

Needless to say, there was very little appreciation for the Blessed Virgin Mary in me, let alone an urge to follow her example. I had no personal connection to Mary save that I had inherited my grandmother's Rosary beads. (I had little gratitude for that gift until years later.)

From the gospel accounts, I knew Mary was necessary for the Incarnation to take place so that Jesus, who is God, could become a man. Mary also showed up at the foot of the Cross when Jesus died. Other than that, Mary and I had a passing acquaintance. I saw her as a religious figure in history rather than someone significant to me.

I loved Jesus although I lived as if Mary, his mother, were optional. She was outside my radar. I dismissed her as unnecessary to my spiritual growth and life. Jesus was enough for me.

My dulled ideas about Mary came through the opinions of others. It was like I believed gossip about Mary, never giving her the benefit of the doubt. Looking back and pondering Mary's role in my life now, I regret my mistakes. I would never want people to trust gossip or falsehoods about me, but I easily adopted others' opinions of Mary. No questions asked. I claimed I loved scripture, but my impressions were neither rooted in scripture nor Church teaching.

My misconceptions about Mary came from three sources.

First, some Catholics treated Mary as old school, a relic from the past. After Vatican II, in the New York area where I grew up, many churches dropped formal devotions to Mary and the saints. The Rosary and other prayer practices like novenas and chaplets were not emphasized. Basically, I ignored Mary.

Second, there was the feminist argument. What could a first-century Galilean woman possibly have in common with a woman like me? What did Mary know about my life? What did she know about going to college, getting a job, and having to earn a living? After all, she lived in a repressive patriarchal culture. She had no power. These days, women are powerful. We need strong heroines, not "handmaids" as Mary had called herself. I viewed Mary as weak.

The third source of my disregard came from non-Catholic friends and colleagues. A few accused Catholics of worshipping Mary. The Ten Commandments prohibit false gods, and that would include worship of any creature. Since I did not know much about Mary, I could not defend her against such accusations.

Today I know that the Catholic Church teaches that we worship Jesus alone. Mary is not some goddess. She is a flesh-and-blood human creature created by God. Indeed, the Church teaches that Mary worships Jesus like we do. We worship Jesus with Mary and with the saints and angels. The honor we give to Mary and the saints is veneration. Therefore, we hold them with the highest human esteem, with a special kind of devotion and love that is lower than our worship. Adoration is reserved for God alone. Catholics don't pray *to* Mary. Catholics pray *with* Mary. We ask for her intercession, just like we ask a good friend to pray for us and with us.

Eventually, as I pondered my own conversations with Jesus, I learned two things. One, my early ideas about Mary were incorrect. And two, I was ignoring someone Jesus loved.

I began noticing those Bible verses about Mary's ponderings. Mary knew something of prayer, and she knew Jesus in a way I never could. The more I pondered Jesus, the more he found opportunities for me to ponder his mother. And the more I pondered Mary, the more I understood that living from the inside out had a lot to do with considering the things Jesus said and did and taking them to heart as Mary had. Living from the inside out worked best when I was tuned in to what God said about my life. It was like making God the first preset I go to on the radio, the first voice that captures my attention without distraction.

With practice over time, a natural rhythm occurred. Pondering led me to the place of prayer or conversation with God within my inner tabernacle, and prayer led me to ponder the words of God in scripture and through Church teaching. What's more, the invisible inner tabernacle of God's presence in my soul yearned more deeply for the visible tabernacle of God's presence found in the Church and vice versa, as slowly I learned that God's presence had, all along, desired mine.

Chapter 2

God's
Good Opinion
of You

My mother was lucky to have had me, I'm told. Given what I know of my birth, I'd call it being *blessed*.

After the heartbreak of an earlier miscarriage, my mother, fortunately, carried me to full term. Things did not go very smoothly the day Mom went into labor with me. After fourteen arduous hours, the doctor still could not remedy my breeched position. Time was no longer on my side. As my mother was prepped for an emergency caesarian section, the doctor prepared my father for the worst, saying, "We're going to try to save both of them." Gulp.

Looking back, my mother said she thanked God that she had a Catholic doctor whose professional and personal ethics recommended doing everything possible for both mother and baby. I couldn't agree more.

So I entered the world, after giving everyone—Mom, Dad, and the doctor—quite a scare. Knowing my birth story has deepened my gratitude for God's hand in my life from my start.

I was meant to be here, and so are you. We probably could talk about the word *blessed* just in terms of this moment— right now. You're reading this as you breathe in and out. That's a blessing. We are *blessed* that we have simply been called to be. It is worth pondering.

When I count my blessings, my birth starts the list. My traumatic breech birth, medically speaking, probably contributed to my developmental hip dysplasia later in life. But God knew that about me and knew a whole bunch more—all the ups and downs that would happen—and God still thought my life was a good idea. So here I am.

Psalm 139 assures us that God knew us in the womb:

> LORD, you have probed me, you know me . . .
> You formed my inmost being;
> you knit me in my mother's womb.
> I praise you, because I am wonderfully made;
> wonderful are your works!
> My very self you know.
> My bones are not hidden from you,
> When I was being made in secret,
> fashioned in the depths of the earth.
> Your eyes saw me unformed;
> in your book all are written down;
> my days were shaped, before one came to be.
> (Ps 139:1, 13–16 NAB)

Even before my mother knew she was pregnant with me, God knew me. That psalm shows me that my life is a blessing in spite of my difficult arrival. My earliest recall of this psalm was from my high school days. Back then I was young and strong: an athlete, a musician, a rider of horses, and a climber of mountains. I didn't know what it was like to be broken in body or to have physical liabilities.

Given my hip-joint problems, it's no surprise I'm now drawn in by the verse about the bones. God knew that I'd deal with that impairment someday. Even with my physical flaws, I'm grateful God saw fit to fashion me.

To me, Psalm 139 is a love song. The God who knew us in secret had our best interest at heart and a tender concern for the intimate details that define our lives. God wonderfully knit us together in the sanctuary of the womb.

While I was in utero, God saw my whole life stretched before him. All my days were ordained. He foresaw my hectic birth, and he alone knows the day of my death. God knows every day in between. He foresaw the first twinge of pain on the treadmill and the first limp. He saw that and so much more.

God saw my parents and my sisters. God knew my first home, my first school, my future husband and children. God saw it all when I was created. (God even saw this book.)

This makes me glad that I learned Psalm 139 when I was young. Over the years, I've returned to it as a source of comfort. God sees everything—the good, the bad, and the ugly—and he is present to it.

God would see all the way out to a really bad day one May. While I was showering, I found that lump that would be subsequently diagnosed as breast cancer. He knew my fears at age thirty-six. He had already counted how many times I would wonder aloud about the days I might have left.

He could have predicted with accuracy that after fourteen happy years of marriage and three small children, I would gain membership in the club nobody wants to join: the ranks of the seriously ill. God would also see the nights I awoke terrified, fearing I might prematurely leave my husband alone and my children motherless.

God knew me in a way nobody else could when I felt my body—the body that he had knit together—had betrayed me. The baby girl who couldn't find her way out of the womb without an intervention was the same woman staring at the tomb, grappling with a potentially fatal illness and her own mortality. In both cases, my life was saved by medical teams and, I trust, by the healing graces from the One who knew everything about me from the moment I was conceived.

I was being taught what my faith practice had professed for years and what Christians profess all the time in the Nicene Creed: "I believe in the Holy Spirit, the Lord, the giver of life."

I learned that being alive is the first and primordial blessing regardless of the length of days we might have. I also learned that God has a plan for each of those days.

We all know our birth story to some extent. Our early histories may or may not be happy, depending on circumstances. What we do or don't know affects our core understanding of ourselves. We all have to answer the questions of life eventually.

We all need to know *who* we are. We all need to answer the important question, "Who am I?" The sooner we can accept the truth about ourselves, that is, God's good opinion of us, the better.

Just as we all have a birth story, we have a conception story. Yet even our own parents do not know the exact moment when we were conceived. They may have an idea of the date or the setting, but for all our scientific knowledge about biology and genetics, we really don't know the exact moment of our own conception. Only God can name the true moment.

For each one of us was created at a precise, unrepeatable moment when God said *yes* to our being. God ordained all of our days in that nanosecond. God's knowledge of us is so intimate and powerful that he can point to that fixed and unique moment in history when we came to be. One moment we did not exist. The next moment we did. That moment was a complete and utter blessing.

In other words, God knows who we are. Pope Benedict XVI preached that "each of us is the result of a thought of God" (*Homily*, April 24, 2005).

God knows us deeper than the cellular level where sperm and ova meet. God knows us where the spiritual and physical collide, where the tinder of the body meets the spark of the soul in a brilliant, ecstatic flash of his unapproachable immortal light and genius. God's design of us in the sanctuary of our mother's womb knitted together a body and an immortal soul.

Whether we choose to believe the truth of our creation as told in God's Word in the poetry of Psalm 139 or we look to the majesty of modern biology to understand the blessing of when our life began, the result is the same. We come to the truth that we did not create ourselves.

God wanted us to know that he knows us and that he called us into being. Why would God want that?

Let's start here: everything about our life and dignity flows from the Holy Trinity; God is one God in three persons: the Father, the Son, and the Holy Spirit. For Catholics, this is a familiar reality because the Trinity is the center of our faith as professed in our Creed.

In the Creed, we first acknowledge the Father almighty as the Maker or Creator of all: "I believe in one God, the Father almighty, maker of heaven and earth, of all things visible and invisible." We profess God the Father as the source of all life. Nothing exists without him. However, our existence, while universally from God, is remarkably personal as well. We've already seen that we all have different birth stories. But only God knows our personal conception stories, our unique and one-of-a-kind narrative.

God's memory of us is better than a mother's baby book, which is used to chronicle her child's earliest moments. God has given us a recollection, a narrative that applies to every woman and man.

God offers us a universal conception story, aptly opening the first book of the Bible known as Genesis, or "the beginning," where the creation stories are recorded. The *Catechism of the Catholic Church* (CCC) assures us that when we listen "to the message of creation and to the voice of conscience," we can "arrive at certainty about the existence of God, the cause and the end of everything" (*CCC*, 46). In Genesis, God describes the creation of man and woman. It is there that we find a remarkable dignity spelled out in how we came to be. We were first conceived in the heart of God and then given life on the earth.

Most of us are familiar with the creation story in the first chapter of Genesis. Within days, God creates the universe and the world with all the lands and seas, flora and fauna. Immediately following that, God creates people. Let's listen in to the start of a conversation between the members of the Trinity as found in Genesis: "Then God said, 'Let us make man in our image, after our likeness'" (Gn 1:26).

Look at the key pronouns in that sentence: "Let *us* make man in *our* image, after *our* likeness." The voice of God speaks as a plural. Do you see and hear the voice of the Trinity coming through? This is the three-persons-in-one God conversing. It illustrates the relationship between the three persons of the Trinity.

In the creation of human beings, the Trinity images itself: "So God created man in his own image, in the image of God he created him; male and female he created them" (Gn 1:27). How remarkable! God creates people resembling him in some way. There is some tangible evidence in our creation that reflects God. The resemblance, or imaging, takes two forms: male and female. We can discern equality with one another, male and female, though a differentiation. Just as in the Trinity itself, there is equality among persons, yet there is differentiation.

Both male and female possess something of the image of God in their design, and on this their dignity rests. Being made in the image of God is an amazing concept. It is here we find the dignity inherent in our very being, in our bodies and in our souls. "And God saw everything that he had made, and behold, it was very good" (Gn 1:31).

Got that? We are good.

Here we find the origin and truth about ourselves. At the moment of our conception, at our creation, God determined our femininity or masculinity. Both are very good. Men and women are equal in being made with the same human nature, yet they are distinct in their bodies. What's more, such distinctions are made to engender complementarity between the sexes—not competition. Men and women, while being distinct, are equal in the eyes of God.

For women who have been made to feel inferior or who have suffered unjustly at the hands of others because of their femininity, this is very good news. This is the truth God has always intended us to believe about ourselves. God designed us and called us into being. He chose femininity for us, and we are very good.

This is a concept that is worth dwelling on, putting aside negatives that reduce our dignity or strip us of self-worth. Regardless of family history, God loves us and willed us into being. We were no accident, for God conceived of us in love. You and I are—and always have been—wanted by God.

Our goodness, our true dignity, is grounded in our being, in being *who* we are. Being created as a woman is our beatitude, our supreme blessedness, because it comes with God's first blessing, the blessing of life.

Being a woman is very good. God effectively says *yes* to the blessing of our being and to our feminine sex. For our part, we may not have always said *yes* to our feminine self, or perhaps our feminine soul has been belittled or abused by people or circumstances beyond our control. But we are not beyond the sight and reach of God who knew us in our mother's womb and who knows the one thing about us that nobody else knows: our genesis.

God saw every woman he has made . . . and behold, she is very good.

You are very good.

When we accept that, we can recover from whatever counterfeits we have bought or believed about ourselves. In comprehending having been made in the image of God, we come to understand *who* we are and *whose* we are. God reveals his love for us in the way we've been made. God has a stake in us, a desire that we might be like him. Being created in the image of God also signals what we might naturally do.

Following the creation of man and woman, the word *blessing* appears in the Bible for the first time. It is the blessing God gives to the man and woman in the garden: "And God blessed them, and God said to them, 'Be fruitful and multiply, and fill the earth and subdue it; and have dominion over [it]'. . . . And it was so. And God saw everything that he had made, and behold, it was very good" (Gn 1:28, 30, 31).

God initiates the relationship with the man and the woman and converses with them. Then God *blesses* them. They are the crowning glory of his creation. After blessing them, implying their marital union, God gives them instructions to "be fruitful and multiply," thereby placing the man and woman in relationship with one another. In this way, the first couple is to have a share in God's creative genius. They are also instructed to be in relationship with creation. They become stewards over all that God has made and provided. Finally, the man and woman, as well as their relationship with each other and with creation, are declared to be "very good."

Are we noticing a pattern of goodness? Can we perceive God's good opinion of us through his creation of human persons? God doesn't just declare us good; God calls us to be good and to foster goodness in our relationships, too. Certainly, we reflect the image of the Trinity when we engage in life-giving relationships.

We women "get" this relationship thing. We intuitively know that we thrive when we experience good relationships with God and others. A woman's happiness is in forming and lovingly tending to her relationships. Honestly, I think the healthier relationships we have are directly proportional to the influence we allow the Trinity to have in our lives.

Let me explain.

Tucked in the *Catechism of the Catholic Church* is a very powerful paragraph telling of the nature of the Trinity. The paragraph indicates that because God has sent his son Jesus and his Holy Spirit into the world, God has revealed his innermost secret. God has an innermost secret? And it's already been revealed? In case we missed the memo, the catechism explains:

> God's very being is love. By sending his only Son and
> the Spirit of Love . . . God has revealed his innermost
> secret. God himself is an eternal exchange of love, Father,
> Son and Spirit, and he has destined us to share in that
> exchange. (CCC, 221)

God himself is an eternal "exchange of love"—among each member of the Trinity, one to another—like a loving family. The fullness of love between the Father, Son, and Spirit goes around and around. It never tires, it never empties, it never ends.

> The Father gives himself completely to the Son, holding
> nothing back; the Son returns this gift in infinite love and
> gratitude. So real and life-giving is their communion that
> it eternally springs forth in the third Person of the Trinity,
> the Holy Spirit. (Mary Healy, *Men and Women Are from
> Eden: A Study Guide to John Paul II's Theology of the Body*
> [Cincinnati: Servant, 2005], 16)

For all eternity, the Trinity has existed as an eternal exchange of selfless love. God exists as a family of persons or a communion of persons. God is all about "relationship." St. John told us succinctly in the often-quoted words, "God is love" (1 Jn 4:8).

So if we are made in the image of God, whose innermost secret is being an eternal exchange of love, what might our lives be called to reflect?

We image the Trinity best when our lives become an exchange of love, when we give love and receive love, in a communion of persons. Masculinity and femininity have natural aspects engendering us to become people of love, of fruitful relationships. A woman is blessed from her gendered body and soul to her predisposition to receive love and to give love, both to God and other people.

Besides this blessed identity of being made in the image of God, a woman is doubly blessed because she has a destiny: heaven. Our existence points to our destiny. God desires that we be joined to him forever. When God spoke his *yes* to create us, he spoke it for eternity.

Now, if this is the true dignity of women—what went wrong? Why have women suffered so in the history of the world?

It all started with the first broken relationship. Readers of Genesis will know that soon after the creation of man and woman, there was the fall. The first sin, or original sin, occurred after the man and woman doubted and disobeyed God, after being tempted by the serpent. They ate the forbidden fruit:

> So when the woman saw that the tree was good for food, and that it was a delight to the eyes, and that the tree was to be desired to make one wise, she took of its fruit and ate; and she also gave some to her husband, and he ate. Then the eyes of both were opened. (Gn 3:6–7)

Adam and Eve's sin was a failure to trust that God had their best interest at heart. This was the same God who had designed them in his image, given them an inspiring complementarity, and furnished a home of intoxicating beauty in paradise.

This broke God's heart, though he saw it coming. Their actions were more than the breaking of a rule in the legal sense, though it was that. More than that, this sin severed the first couple's relationship with a loving God, and it fractured their own relationship.

As if something other than God could satisfy her, Eve doubted God's goodness and succumbed first. Adam sinned, too, moments later. Tempted though they were by the devil disguised as a serpent, they committed the sin, and the sin brought severe consequences in the life of the man and woman. They were created to be immortal with preternatural gifts such as infused knowledge. In the aftermath of sin, their bodies grew old and decayed, and their consciences dimmed. Paradise was lost. The man and woman were separated from God in a way that pretty much sums up the state of humanity today. Every future man and woman lives with the effects of the original sin.

Yet, hope was never fully lost. God foresaw the day that he would send his son as the Savior.

God's plan for redemption began with a woman. The Savior of the world, promised immediately after the fall, would come through a new woman at a turning point in history to do battle again with the devil:

> The LORD God said to the serpent, "Because you have done this, cursed are you . . . upon your belly you shall go, and dust you shall eat all the days of your life. I will put enmity between you and the woman, and between your seed and her seed; he shall bruise your head, and you shall bruise his heel." (Gn 3:14–15)

Scripture scholars see these verses predicting the son (Jesus) of a woman (Mary) who would offer a mortal blow to the head of the serpent (the devil).

This is why the dignity of womanhood is most perfectly reflected in Mary. Her vital role in salvation history brings

Jesus, God's son, into the world. Mary is not just a biological necessity for the Incarnation. No. Through Mary, God brought forth a profound recasting of the glory of being a woman—a woman whose virginity and maternity brought new light, love, and life to the world.

Why was this significant for the dignity of women? God turned to a woman to set things right. Ever since Genesis recorded Eve's infamous transgression with Adam, original sin cast a long and enduring shadow over the human race. Centuries of distrust, dismissal, and discrimination toward women followed. That sinful condition negatively influenced every human creature ever born, save one.

Enter Mary.

A radical new order emerged with the conception of Mary in her mother's womb. God prepared her conception to be immaculately pure in body and soul. God did this so Jesus would come into the world through Mary by the power of the Holy Spirit. The son of God's human conception would take place in her womb, with her loving consent. (See Lk 1:26–35.)

Mary becomes the womanly antidote for the poison and sad posterity spread from Eve's mistake. In Mary, God underscores the dignity he always longed for women to enjoy since humankind's beginning, described in Genesis.

Mary's conception—her creation—is the masterpiece, the zenith of God's creation. She, the sinless virgin, is the highest creature. She is not the sad posterity of Eve. Mary's obedience defies the devil, and her son, Jesus, crushes him.

In the second century, St. Irenaeus wrote, "The knot of Eve's disobedience was untied by Mary's obedience: what the virgin Eve bound through her disbelief, Mary loosened by her faith" (CCC, 494).

Mary became the greatest woman (ever) for two reasons: her very being was immaculate, or sinless, and she willingly cooperated with God's plan. We have not heard this enough: Mary dispels all the negative echoes and persistent falsehoods that demean or disrespect women as being less than men or that describe women as somehow doomed or disgraced by their sex.

> *In Mary, Eve discovers* the nature of the true dignity of woman, of feminine humanity. This discovery must continually reach the heart of every woman and shape her vocation and her life. (John Paul II, *Mulieris Dignitatem*, 11)

Thanks to Mary, our identity as women is good, indeed, very good. Yes, it's even blessed.

In the end, I dropped my negative opinions about Mary because of God's good opinion of her. My misconceptions have been replaced with awe of Mary, the immaculate conception, the promised woman of God conceived without sin.

The entire Trinity has a sublime love of Mary. She is daughter of the Father, mother to the Son, and spouse of the Holy Spirit. In Mary, we see how a woman's love and life are vital to God's plan. If God loves Mary, we can, too. Indeed, the reverse is also true. Mary can be the bridge for our healthy relationships with each member of the Trinity. Befriending her is a good thing.

Chapter 3

Your
Soul's
Tattoo

Are you a beloved daughter?

It's an identity question that stirs up a host of feelings, memories, or quandaries, depending on who is being asked and who is doing the asking. That's because we often identify our belovedness circumstantially. All women are daughters. That much is certain. But our backgrounds differ. We have positive and negative relationships and experiences that may affect our answer.

Are you a beloved daughter of God?

That adds an order of magnitude to the question that may be helpful in answering the first question. I would suggest that this second question about being a beloved daughter of

God is the larger reality, the fuller truth. It not only encompasses the first question, but it settles it.

To be a beloved daughter is a blessing. It indicates being chosen, being highly regarded, and being much loved. A beloved daughter can identify herself because she trusts the love of her parents for her. A beloved daughter of God understands and trusts her sacred identity and calling in light of her Baptism. If that describes you, you already possess a deep blessing.

If you are a woman who feels like she's failed to get the message regarding this blessing, you are not alone. Many of us carry emotional wounds that better describe our brokenness as daughters rather than our belovedness.

So let's talk about that deep place in every woman's heart that longs for the dignity of being beloved. Let's move toward seeking that blessing. Personal, emotional wounds are tough to talk about. Let's face it: nobody is immune from hurts. Some hurts are self-inflicted. Many are caused by the words and actions of others. Some are a combination of the two.

Claiming our identity as beloved daughters—in God's eyes—can be difficult and hampered, or it can be nurtured and embraced, due to circumstances in our families of origin. Our families, for better or worse, are the places where our impressions are born regarding the relationships of father, mother, sister, and brother. All these relationships impact, in due time, our relationship with the family of God. Of course, I'm referring both to God in the Trinity—Father, Son, and Spirit—and in our connection to the family of God, the Church. It is important that we pause here to talk about the place that the fatherhood of God has in our lives.

Every daughter has an earthly father. Fatherhood matters to us. A father's presence in our lives has impact, for good or for ill.

One of the benefits of midlife for me is having enough life experience to know that God can bring good out of a bad situation, eventually (see Rom 8:28; 2 Cor 4:17–18). And, though it's hard to admit, we can learn and grow through heartaches.

I didn't have that mature perspective in my early years. I look back to my teen years and find a lot of anger and disappointment in the families around me. When I consider my peer group from those years, I remember a world of hurt where fathers and daughters were concerned. Some of my friends dealt with alcoholic fathers, controlling and angry fathers, and fathers who left their families through abandonment and divorce. There's no shortage of men who give fatherhood a bad name.

I'm not here to criticize parents; they have important roles in light of eternity. God knows my parents weren't perfect, and I'm no perfect parent either. Just ask my kids. They've got stories about how I've blown it with them and how my own quick temper and strong tongue has, ashamedly, done damage.

Poor relationships with an earthly parent can weaken or sever our bond with a heavenly parent. The *Catechism of the Catholic Church* backs me up on this. In fact, the Church takes a consoling view toward those who have suffered emotional wounds from parents. When we experience hurt with our earthly parents, it can mar our relationship with God. That shows you the magnitude of a parent's influence! In particular, the Church acknowledges that parental love, or its absence, has a deep and profound effect on the way children will respond to God as a father.

Why would the Church care about that?

First, because the Trinity is made up of family ties—Father, Son, and Spirit. And second, you cannot be a practicing Catholic for any length of time and not encounter the truth of the matter: our biblical and liturgical expressions (the Creed, the Our Father at Mass, and elsewhere) look to God as Father. The Church intends for us to relate to God in exactly that way because Jesus did.

The *Catechism of the Catholic Church* offers hope to those who experience brokenness in their father-daughter relationship:

> Parents . . . are in a way the first representatives of God for man. But this experience also tells us that human parents are fallible and can disfigure the face of father-hood and motherhood . . . Recall that God transcends the human distinction between the sexes. He is neither man nor woman: he is God. He also transcends human fatherhood and motherhood, although he is their origin and standard: no one is father as God is Father. (*CCC*, 239)

The fatherhood of God is bigger than our perceptions distorted by hurt and pain. God's love transcends those hurts, for we are children of God. Our dignity as women is that we are daughters of God, but we may not always know it.

I've lived long enough to know that brokenness, brought into the light of love, can become an opportunity for blessing and growth, to learn or relearn belovedness.

There come times in every Christian's life when we have to reconcile the truths of what we profess to believe with the way we are actually living. The Church calls this move-ment *ongoing conversion*. It is a realignment of our ways with God's ways, of acknowledging *whose* we are. We are works in progress, and our lives should be moving in a direction of ever-deepening relationships with God and others. Yet, there are times and places when we are stalled or stuck or fright-ened. We long to move forward, to seek a remedy, to repair the broken track that is derailing our hearts. One example of this kind of reconciling in my own heart took place during my engagement to Bob. It was a lesson in learning to become the beloved daughter of God.

Bob and I entered into the required premarital preparations with a wonderful priest-counselor. Have I mentioned being given to a kind of short-temperedness? Well, the first time I had to come squarely face-to-face with this flaw in myself was in those counseling sessions. This very fatherly priest called me out. He knew my weaknesses would have ramifications in our marriage—not to mention the trickle-down effect on our future children. As I confronted this deficit in myself, I discovered I had adopted a dim view of fatherly correction.

In my teen years, when my dad and I disagreed, being of a similar temperament, we did so loudly. I'm not proud of it. But there you have it. Being quick-tempered and having friends with their own father issues didn't help me respect the proper authority a father should have in my life. My heart had developed a credibility gap where God the Father was concerned. But just as I had a few bad habits, one good habit saved me: I had learned to pray using the words of the Bible and the words of the Mass when my own words failed me.

Jesus used this engagement period to work on these things within me because they boiled down to whether or not I would trust the fatherhood of God for myself and, eventually, trust my husband with the fatherhood of our children within our marriage.

The first step in my growth was acknowledging the bigness of God. The creedal prayer "I believe in one God the Father almighty" allowed me to start to trust my Father in heaven who is a big God. God was bigger than any problems I had—bigger than my fears about our future parenting and bigger than my wrestling match with anger in myself. And his plan was greater than my own.

I pondered my earliest beginnings.

Father God had used my parents in his designing of me, calling me into being. God used my mom and dad to bring me into this world, to give me the gift of life, and to raise me. Their faith brought me, as an infant, to the church for Baptism. I was already blessed by being created in the image of God, yet a deeper blessing awaited me in my Baptism. In preparing for Matrimony, I reviewed all the sacraments I had already received. I was struck by how little I knew about them.

Over time, I found a key that I didn't know I needed. I had failed to embrace my deepest identity as a baptized person. Whether we know it or not, our Baptism is the deepest grace of our lives. It is the foundation on which all other sacraments are built.

Baptism begins with God's first love of us—a love born in the midst of the Trinity—and spills over to us. And we recall that the Trinity is all about relationships, right?

For the moment, let's just focus on Jesus because Jesus is the link that enables the father-daughter thing to work. God desired and pursued a relationship with us. The entire Old Testament of scripture is HIS-story, the story of God's wooing and demonstrative love that crescendos in the coming of God himself as one of us.

T. S. Eliot describes it as "the still point of the turning world" (T. S. Eliot, *Four Quartets* [New York: Harcourt and Brace, 1943], line 64). It happens in the Incarnation of Christ, the arrival of Jesus on earth as a man. The Son of God becomes a son of Mary. In Mary, heaven and earth meet.

Jesus entered into the world that we might enter into relationship with God the Father. We all need to know who our

Father is. "For God so loved the world that he gave his only Son, so that everyone who believes in him should not perish but have eternal life" (Jn 3:16).

Maybe you've heard that before. Sometimes when we hear something over and over again, we take it for granted. Notice the language of fatherhood, love, and life: "For *God* so *loved* . . . that *he* gave *his* only *Son*. . . . Everyone who believes in him should . . . have eternal *life*."

Jesus is God's love song. He woos a daughter's heart to the Father. Jesus reveals the personal and unique love God has for us and his universal plan of love for the salvation of the world. Jesus taught us about God in the ways we really need to experience him most—as a father.

Jesus knows some of us harbor reticence when it comes to fatherhood. Still Jesus teaches the necessity of our knowing the Father: "I and the Father are one" (Jn 10:30). He reveals the Father by what he did and said. He never stops using examples in parables about fathers or praying to the Father himself.

The gospels record Jesus saying the word *father* over 130 times. Coming to know the Father in heaven is not optional for a Christian. Jesus repairs the rift opened in the days of Adam and Eve when the first human relationships with the Father were fractured. Most important, Jesus instructed us to call God "Our Father" in The Lord's Prayer, which is one of the most basic prayers in Christianity: "*Our Father*, who art in heaven, Hallowed be thy name" (Mt 6:9; emphasis added).

Jesus taught us how to enter into his prayer, using his words, when he taught us to pray to our Father. Jesus shares the love of his Father so that we, too, might enter into conversations and prayers—a loving relationship—with the Father like he did. Ultimately, "the Lord's Prayer *reveals us to ourselves* at the same time that it reveals the Father to us" (*CCC*, 2783).

The gospels are filled with Jesus's prayers to the Father, a Father that yearns to love us, not disappoint or hurt us, a loving Father who understands the baggage we may be carrying. Let's make Jesus's words our own. Learning the words of the Son's heart can help heal our daughter hearts.

The image of the Good Shepherd soothes my daughter heart. Jesus describes the tender, committed care that he offers his sheep, a care in union with his Father:

> My sheep hear my voice, and I know them, and they follow me; and I give them eternal life, and they shall never perish, and no one shall snatch them out of my hand. My Father, who has given them to me, is greater than all, and no one is able to snatch them out of the Father's hand. I and the Father are one. (Jn 10:27–30)

No one is father as God is Father. If someone has treated you badly, such that you cannot understand the gift of the Father's love, remember that "no one is able to snatch . . . [you] out of the Father's hand." His love for you has never wavered, even if you have been unable to know it, see it, or understand it. Jesus's word guarantees it.

We can make this our prayer, too: no one can snatch me out of the Father's hand.

To trust Jesus is to trust the Father.

When we address God as our Father, as Jesus has taught, we are moved toward trusting the Father. When we refer to God as "our Father," we do two important things. First, we declare him as the origin of everything in our lives. Second, we trust the goodness and loving care that a father bestows. (See *CCC*, 239.)

When Jesus was finished with his work on earth, he charged his followers to baptize in the name of the Father, the Son, and the Holy Spirit. (See Mt 28:18–20.)

In the graces of Baptism, God became a father to me. I was born into the family of God, and the love of the Trinity was extended to me by name—Patricia Ann—baptized in the name of the Father, Son, and Spirit. Of course, I was an infant at the time, and still, Baptism was and is a great gift that my parents obtained for me. Baptism secured my dignity as a beloved daughter and brought healing to my life. The graces of Baptism empower me to make Jesus's words my own. As I said before, when she knows she is beloved, a daughter can trust the father's love. It is a deep blessing. *Whose* we are matters.

In Baptism we meet the fatherhood of God, blessed and dignified as beloved daughters. Unfortunately, it is a gift we can fail to recognize or take for granted. Imagine owning a costly heirloom worth millions but having no idea of its value because it is locked away in a chest and forgotten. For many of us, that treasure is our Baptism, specifically the knowledge that we are God's beloved daughters. That knowledge is the key that unlocks many graces.

In Baptism, we are made for holiness. We are brought into the family of God. We are yoked to God, a Blessed Trinity of Father, Son, and Holy Spirit. We are daughters of a loving Father who is perfect and transcendent beyond our earthbound impressions. He always knows what's best for his daughters. If we ponder that, relying on the graces we've already received in Baptism, we will begin to reclaim the girl who may be carrying around a lot of angst and rejection where fatherhood is concerned.

Baptized Christians utter the word *Father* six times in the Nicene Creed. There's a reason. We are blessed daughters standing before a magnificent, loving, all-knowing Father. Plus, the Creed spells out our belief and relationship with the three-in-one God.

We are a sister and friend to Jesus Christ, a most sublime, supernatural-yet-approachable brother. In Jesus, we see the invisible Father. The Savior who died for our sins reversed the curse imposed at Eden after the fall. Jesus is the truest friend we will ever have. Read the gospels and see his respect for every woman he has ever met, breaking with the social conventions of his day.

Finally, we are consecrated witnesses to the Spirit. The Searcher of Hearts, the Source of All Wisdom, and the Giver of Life abides in the tabernacle of our soul. By extension, we are baptized into the Church, the family of God on earth, together with saints in heaven. This familial relationship with God is the truth of our dignity, our beatitude, and beatitude is supreme blessedness.

Everyone wants to find happiness, right? Blessedness is church-speak for happiness. You are extremely blessed. You belong to God. You were made for truth. You were made for goodness. You were made to know beauty.

You are beautiful. You are loved.

You are unrepeatable, unique, valuable.

You are sacred in God's eyes.

You are sacred.

You.

You didn't earn it. It was free. You have a link to God that you didn't create. It flows from the lavishness of God's love. Your worth, in his eyes, is priceless. The prophet says that God considers you "the apple of his eye" (Zec 2:8).

Baptism reveals our true dignity as children, beloved of God. That's our beatitude, our blessedness.

Once we trust this Baptism, once we delight in it and claim it—this relationship with God we were destined to have—God will transform our lives. In Baptism, a remarkable thing occurred. God took up residence in us: "Christ in you, the hope of glory" (Col 1:27). Not only did the God of the universe create us in his image, not only does he want us to be like him, God actually wants to live *in us*.

Baptism purifies us from all sins and makes us "a new creation" in Christ (2 Cor 5:17). Baptized in the name of the Trinity, you have a profound three-fold dignity as a daughter of God, a co-heir with Christ, and a temple of his Holy Spirit (cf. 1 Cor 6:15, 19; 12:27; Rom 8:17. (See CCC, 1265.)

Baptismal grace enables us to believe in God and supplies the power to live in harmony with the prompting voice of the Holy Spirit. These graces are divine assistance to trust God, to be good, and to do good. Grace builds up our faith, strengthens our hope, and deepens our love, equipping us with moral virtues, the compass for our conscience.

Remember the sanctity of your conscience, that place where you live with God? This is where God's love enters in. Here the fatherhood of God heals our hurts. Lest we think this is some kind of romanticized vision of love, think again. It is rugged and strongly tempered in power, yet gentle and approachable enough to trust. The Father's love is sturdy enough to enable us not only to thrive despite our hurts, but also to transcend them.

How can we transcend hurts? You already know—by deeply entering into the prayers of Jesus and making them your own. Jesus and our Baptism give us direct access to our heavenly Father. You've seen it with the Our Father; now take it a step deeper. Jesus prayed at his crucifixion amidst complete suffering. He forgave his persecutors, his detractors, enemies, friends who betrayed or left him, and those who forcibly put him to death. And he forgave us even before we came to be: "And Jesus said, 'Father, forgive them'" (Lk 23:34).

With grace, we can forgive in the name of Jesus, with Jesus, who is one with the Father. I can forgive each person who has hurt me, even the worst offenders. I can even forgive myself. "Father, forgive them." Father, forgive me.

The name of the Father is the name Jesus used when his deepest wounds were open and bleeding. It's the name we can call on to heal us of wounds we can see and the ones we keep hidden. It's the name that brings our ongoing conversion.

If we have lived like a prodigal daughter, we can turn our hearts back toward the Father who longs to receive us. The Father's love will lead us home. Jesus's parable of the prodigal son—it has often been said—should be renamed "The Forgiving Father." (See Lk 15:11–32.)

Baptism is the gateway for the healing graces found in other sacraments. The sacrament of Reconciliation repairs our brokenness with God and strengthens our identity as beloved. No woman's heart is beyond the Father's love. If you've lost touch with trusting his fatherly care, make this a conversation with a priest in the privacy of confession. You will reclaim the blessing of your dignity.

Baptism begins a lifelong conversation with Christ and the Church, inviting us to become saints. As saints, we resemble Christ while maintaining our distinctive qualities to become our truest selves.

Baptism, like our creation, shapes our identity and destiny. It tells us who we are, where we came from, and where we are going: God is our origin and our end. It defines where home is and where we belong. It sets the course for the rest of life—and eternity—if we embrace it. We must choose to live the glory of our Baptism.

Baptism reminds us that God sure is crazy about us and not afraid to show it. His attachment to us is intentional, deep, and permanent. Indeed, it's like a lover tattooing a beloved's name on his arm. Only, in our case, God has branded us, placing his loving indelible mark on our souls, like a soul tattoo, claiming us as his own:

> Incorporated into Christ by Baptism, the person baptized is configured to Christ. Baptism seals the Christian with the indelible spiritual mark (*character*) of his belonging to Christ. . . .
>
> The Holy Spirit has marked us with the *seal of the Lord* (*"Dominicus character"*) "for the day of redemption." (CCC, 1272, 1274)

God configures us to be like Christ, the beloved Son. We are beloved daughters not only like Jesus in identity, but also in action. We are called to behave like him, too. Like spiritual DNA, grace enables us to forgive, to reconcile, to heal, and ultimately love like Jesus.

We. Were. Made. For. This.

We were made to be in this intimate relationship with a God who is our Father and who sees himself in us. God delights in us the way parents find joy in a child who resembles them in eye color, shares their love of music, or inherits their taste for cheesecake. Still, it is this and so much more. As John Paul II indicated in his World Youth Day homily, *"We are not the sum of our weaknesses and failures;* we are the sum of the Father's love for us and our real capacity to become the image of his Son"* (July 28, 2002).

Again, Mary offers clues for living as a beloved daughter, for she trusts God completely. Yet, even with Mary, the Father made the first move. He blessed her with singular grace at her immaculate conception, equipping her to respond when he called.

> The angel Gabriel was sent from God . . . to a virgin betrothed to . . . Joseph . . . and the virgin's name was Mary. And he came to her and said, "Hail, O favored one, the Lord is with you! . . . But she was greatly troubled at the saying, and considered in her mind what sort of greeting this might be. And the angel said to her, "Do not be afraid, Mary, for you have found favor with God. And behold, you will conceive in your womb and bear a son, and you shall call his name Jesus. . . . And Mary said, "Behold, I am the handmaid of the Lord; let it be to me according to your word." (Lk 1:26–31, 38)

God the Father trusted Mary. Mary, in turn, trusted the Father and his plan. God's plan of salvation hinged on Mary's trust: "Let it be to me according to your word." The still point in the turning world was found in Mary's *fiat*, her *yes* to God. Mary is the first person since Eve to trust all God planned to bestow, that is, his very self:

> Before anyone else it was God himself, the Eternal Father, who entrusted himself to the Virgin of Nazareth, giving her his own Son in the mystery of the Incarnation.
>
> Mary . . . sheds light on womanhood. . . . Women, by looking to Mary, find in her the secret of living their femininity with dignity and of achieving their own true advancement. (John Paul II, *Redemptoris Mater*, 39, 46)

Mary is a beloved daughter who is a true disciple. The *fiat* is our Christian prayer, one we should enter into ourselves "to be wholly God's, because he is wholly ours" (*CCC*, 2617). When we give our *yes* to God, we make him wholly ours: "My beloved is mine, and I am his" (Sg 2:16).

Finally, as St. Louis de Montfort taught, "The salvation of the whole world began with the Hail Mary. Hence the salvation of each person is also attached to this prayer."

Entering into the Hail Mary, may we imitate Mary, blessed among women, embracing the blessing of our own belovedness. May we, like she, have the graces to receive the plans God entrusts to our care.

Conclusion to Part One

God's plan for us started with our creation and our Baptism. These unchanging realities—being created in the image of God and being baptized in the name of God—are the truth of *who we are* and *whose we are*. They connect us to God in the Holy Trinity, our family, and the Church.

If you were a globe, the sphere of your life—your world—would revolve on the axis stretched between these two poles of being a woman and being a Christian. There is an undeniable gravitational pull—an incredible dignity—between these two unchanging realities that, like your body and soul, form the whole of you.

Our creation and Baptism are the true universal sources of our dignity. They naturally and supernaturally equip us to love and serve others because we can draw deeply from the core truth inside of us: from our very beginnings, we have been loved.

God has given us a mighty *yes*, a *yes* that says we were born for a reason. We, in turn, might say *yes* to knowing and loving him and to living to love others.

What a sublime dignity we have in our God-given identity and destiny. We are *blessed*!

Part Two

THE BEAUTIFUL
GIFTS OF WOMEN

Gifts.

Who doesn't love receiving or giving a beautiful gift?

Women have received remarkable gifts. It is common to think of unique and personal gifts as things that might be natural—creativity, athleticism, intellectual acuity, business savvy, domesticity, and artistic talent. There are traits of temperament, character, and personality that are considered gifts—a sense of humor, compassion, empathy, leadership, service, patience, and self-discipline. There are spiritual gifts—wisdom, understanding, counsel, knowledge, fortitude, piety, and fear of the Lord. (See Is 11:2.)

Notice that when discussing the beautiful gifts of women I have failed so far to discuss their beauty in terms of physical beauty or physique—how a woman looks, her outward adornments, physical attributes, self-expression, or sense of vogue and glamour. That's because this book is focusing on living from the inside out. It's not that we are ignoring those externals. Many of them are governed by our conscience, by our individual tastes and choices that come from inside. And, yes, even these externals have the power to communicate and reflect our dignity and how strongly we perceive our being blessed.

We know that people may judge us, rightly and wrongly, by skin-deep externals. We suffer separations and hurts from other people based on those judgments. We endure painful disappointments over what we think are failings or envy over what we perceive as the abundance of others. Sometimes it is hard to find a point of connection among ourselves and others unless we look to the unchanging dignity found in each unique person. We've already covered the blessing of our unrepeatable dignity in Part One. Now, in Part Two, we'll discuss our womanhood in terms of four universal qualities innate in every woman, inherent in her nature.

These four dynamic gifts characterize the beauty of womanhood: receptivity, generosity, sensitivity, and maternity. With these four universal gifts—attributes or qualities of femininity—women become remarkable gift givers. These four dynamic gifts, magnified by the grace of Baptism and the other sacraments, empower women to make gifts of themselves to God and to other people.

These universal gifts serve to unite women in a sisterhood, where they can befriend one another without the subjective competitiveness emerging from envy or conceit. There are no haves or have-nots.

Together with our inherent dignity, these are gifts that women can and should affirm in one another. These gifts are inborn qualities for living from the inside out, and they help us see and celebrate womanhood in ourselves and in one another.

When we recover a sense of our own beauty through the beautiful gifts we possess, coupled with our blessed dignity, we stand on an unshakable truth that becomes the foundation for understanding our own beauty and the goodness we can bring to God and others through these gifts.

What's more, the unique and personal gifts we each have become even brighter when we use them within the strength of these universals.

Chapter 4

Saying
Yes
to Love

Receptivity. Now there's a word I had never heard growing up. Had I heard it, I probably would have thought it referred to the power of my radio's antenna to pull in strong reception or good signals, as opposed to a beautiful gift that women possess by virtue of being created female. It is the beautiful warmth of femininity that receives and accepts another person or the strong softness that a woman brings to love, of drawing another close to her heart.

Back then the cultural milieu taught many of us to toughen up or even close up—the exact opposite of receptivity. The signals my emotional antenna picked up were negative and did not always make me feel valued as a woman.

The sexual revolution and the feminist movement were in full swing when I was coming of age. It was hard to ignore that many women felt *less than*. I overheard plenty of complaining from my fellow females, from the recurring jokes about the monthly curse of menstruation to the fact that double standards were *de rigueur*. There was not always equal pay for equal work. Working in the late seventies and eighties meant I was subject to sexual harassment more than once, as there were no laws against it. Feminism seemed to be a good in society to correct these injustices.

Today much has changed for women in the workplace and elsewhere, but back in the day, I picked up an attitude that tried to disarm the notions about women being less than men, and it went something like this: "A woman has to be twice as good as a man to be thought of as half as good," and "the best man for the job is a woman."

You get the picture.

Much of my womanly identity became caught up in my need to achieve and to be thought of as good enough. So I sought to achieve things. I became an honor student in high school and college. I played sports competitively, and I worked that way, too. I blazed my own trail. I was the first person, the first woman, in my family to earn a four-year degree. Locally, I was the first woman in retail in a camping department filled with men, courtesy of my years in scouting. After college I worked in radio, where it was still a novelty to have a woman on the air. But I did that, too. I paid my dues and I paid my own way, often with a proverbial chip on my shoulder. I was a strong, educated woman and a leader at my church. But in my quest for success, I had tuned out my feminine gifts as potential liabilities.

Yet glimpses of my receptivity were there. I still loved Jesus. I had a soft spot for the teens I worked with at church and a tall green-eyed musician-turned-electrical-engineer with whom I was slowly falling in love. I had never seen Bob's love coming or marriage fitting in with my ambitions. Up until then, I was a woman in motion: people to see, places to go, things to do. Soon it became clear that I would either marry Bob or let him go. (Back then the thought of living together would never have occurred to us.)

I was a practicing Catholic, so I knew that Christian marriage calls the spouses to put the good of the other ahead of their own. But for a long time, I had really only put myself and my achievements first. Now, don't get me wrong. I'm not discounting my accomplishments or the advancement of women in general. I'm critical of my own self-absorption along the way, hindsight being what it is.

Learning to love Bob is my first vivid recollection of discovering the feminine gift of receptivity in my life, that of receiving another person for his own merits. I discovered I had the capacity to love the goodness in someone with no thought of what I might receive in return. Of course, the reality was that I also was the recipient of his love. That only served to open my heart even more. No longer was I considering just my own singular and narrow pursuits, but trying to be open to a wider vision—maybe God's?

Bob's marriage proposal still surprised me, coming after I returned from a trip to the Midwest to visit friends. I became separated from my luggage and missed my connection. I was stranded alone in a Greyhound bus station in Indianapolis. Feeling lost and being unable to reach my destination, I spent a full day into the night waiting for the next bus. During those lonely hours, in the age long before mobile phones, I kept begging the ticket attendant to make change so that I could pump quarters into the public phone. In my predicament, the only voice I wanted to hear was Bob's. It was there, in a setting devoid of any romance, I realized that Bob was someone I never wanted to live without. My heart was well on its way to receiving his proposal if he asked.

Soon after, Bob did propose in a conversation that referenced my phone calls from the Indiana bus depot, and I accepted. That initial openness to marriage was the gift of my feminine receptivity at work even though I didn't have a name for it at the time. I was still pretty selfishly headstrong, but love was wooing me.

Marriage meant I had to make room for another in my heart and in every other aspect of my life. For all my achievements, nothing had prepared me for what it really meant to receive another person into my life full-time, with a vow to keep that pledge until death. Convinced I was marrying my best friend, I naively figured this kind of sacrificial love for Bob would be easy.

Bob and I married in the fall of 1982, and we selected this Gospel for the nuptial Mass:

> As the Father loves me, so I also love you. Remain in my love.
>
> If you keep my commandments, you will remain in my love, just as I have kept my Father's commandments and remain in his love. I have told you this so that my joy may be in you and your joy may be complete.
>
> This is my commandment: love one another as I love you. No one has greater love than this, to lay down one's life for one's friends. . . .
>
> I have called you friends, because I have told you everything I have heard from my Father.
>
> It was not you who chose me, but I who chose you and appointed you to go and bear fruit that will remain,

so that whatever you ask the Father in my name he may
give you. (Jn 15:9–16 NAB)

These potent words echoed the blessing of being chosen
and loved by God so that we might respond with love for
one another. Bob and I had that scripture reference engraved
inside our wedding rings, though it took years of trial and
error for the truth to become fully inscribed on our hearts.

I learned firsthand that marriage is an amplifier. Everything I liked or disliked about my man before I married
increased in volume after marriage. I ran headlong into a
wall of my selfishness and struggles for power, not to mention my own anger issues that erupted from my quick temper. I struggled with the sacrificial aspects of taking care of
a home and family. Putting others' needs ahead of my own
was harder than I had thought. I bristled when I could not
control things.

Motherhood intensified my struggles, often reducing me
to tears. I was profoundly disappointed with the shortcomings of my love—my lack of achievement! I was trying to
achieve in my marriage and achieve in my mothering the
way I succeeded in school and at work, as if there were a per-
formance scorecard attached to my efforts. "No greater love"
required something more than the tyranny of perfectionism;
it needed my attentiveness, my surrender, and sacrifice. Love
was first more about *being*, rather than *doing*, and putting
people ahead of things. It involved a willingness to just be
in the moment rather than rush past it—receiving instead of
achieving.

I prayed for answers to my small, inadequate love and
my slow interior reception to loving as I ought.

Oh, the lessons of love are easier to inscribe on a ring than
on a life! I relearned them over and over: "As the Father loves

me, so I also love you." I had to enter into that prayer of Jesus and make it my own.

The only cure for too little love is more love. I needed to welcome my family ever deeper into my heart, drawing deeply from the well of God's first love for me. It realigned my thinking to where I could—through my actions to my husband and children—say, "As the Father loves me, so I also love you."

This man and these children aren't a side trip, a detour on the way toward achieving something else. They are the way, the path, and most of all, they are gifts of love. They are gifts of God's love made visible. Bob is a gift. Our children are gifts. I am a gift to them.

But first, I had to receive them as gifts, treasure them as gifts.

Receptivity reflects our dignity and design as women. Our feminine bodies and souls are designed to receive God and others. While I may have been endowed with receptivity, I surely needed lessons in cultivating a spirit of receptivity.

Mary showed me how. I confess, back then, I still struggled with Mary. Old impressions die hard. Why would I want to receive Mary as an example or a mentor for my life? Mary's identifying herself as a *handmaid* had bugged me over the years. After all, it seemed so subservient. "Mary said, 'Behold, I am the handmaid of the Lord. Let it be to me according to your word'" (Lk 1:38).

Ever since marriage and motherhood rocked my world, I had to admire how Mary's self-effacing title of *handmaid* is something she rejoiced in a few verses of Luke later when she praised God for the happiness she had in life: "For he who is mighty has done great things for me, and holy is his name" (Lk 1:49).

Mary responded to God's plan with extraordinary verve and nine unfaltering words: "Let it be to me according to your word" (Lk 1:38).

Were Mary's words relevant to me? Eventually. Marriage and family life had reshaped my life, my plans. What prayer might I enter into to meet the challenges I faced? There was only one: "Let it be to me . . ."

God knew that his power would assist me if I placed my trust, my *yes*, in his providence for my role as a wife and mother, even if in my own weakness I needed to renew that *yes* every day. Whenever I did that, grace flooded in (Jn 15:11). When I trusted God wholeheartedly, I found joy in my role. It's almost as if I could pray alongside Mary that "he who is mighty has done great things for *me*." Indeed, he had. Another lesson was coming alive for me—that God always has our best interest at heart: "I have told you this so that my joy may be in you and your joy may be complete" (Jn 15:11 NAB).

Mary actively and passionately embraced God's plan for her. She willingly chose and trusted what God set out for her to do. Submission to God's plan is anything but a weak choice. In my life, I came to learn that submission puts me under God's mission. Being a loving and faithful servant did not demean Mary; it fulfilled her. As Elizabeth said, "Blessed are you among women" (Lk 1:42), acknowledging Mary's willingness to receive God's plan unselfishly. Mary helped me find the grace I needed to lay down my old self-centered ways in exchange for a new and joyful feminine love that embraced others without fear and without having to receive something in order to give. My *yes* to this vocation revealed my love—the love I gave and received—as gift, not something I earned. It's all a gift. I learned that my struggle wasn't really with Mary at all. It was with humility.

What was it about Mary's humility that I failed to understand? It is that hers is not a powerless humility. But her power is not her own. Mary's humility is filled with the powerful presence of God. Mary is one empowered woman. Her humility is so powerful that it is the correction to Eve's fall, humility being the virtue that acknowledges God is the author of all that is good. Eve's moment of truth occurred when she eagerly grasped at the luscious, though forbidden, fruit. It revealed her doubt that the Father had her best interest at heart, so she took matters into her own hands. Mary, by contrast, in her moment of decision, opened herself up to God's goodness and with open hands received the blessed and more perfect fruit of Jesus.

Power, achievement, and my own gain had quietly underlined much of what I strived for in my young life. I was learning that God's plan required a different kind of empowerment. "It was not you who chose me, but I who chose you and appointed you to go and bear fruit that will "remain" (Jn 15:16 NAB).

In her choosing to be open to the abundant love of God, Mary received the blessing of her identity as a daughter of God. Mary said *yes* to the woman she was designed and destined to be. Mary's *yes*, her "let it be to me" is famously known in the Church as her *fiat*. It was the single greatest moment of loving receptivity the universe has ever known.

As the foundation for receptivity, humility welcomes goodness in love. It is never afraid or suspicious that love will not be enough. God's love is always enough, always abundant.

In God's economy, humility does not belittle Mary's personhood or ours. God only affirms our dignity. Humility is a kind of emptiness that lets receptivity make sense. Humility says to God, "I trust you are good. I am yours. I'm open to your working in me."

Mary received God. She lets him into her heart, her womb, and her whole life. She becomes the womanly embodiment of receptivity in all its forms: biological (womb), emotional (heart), and spiritual (soul). Her receptive nature reveals an active responsiveness to God and others. Mary holds nothing back from God, and God holds nothing back from Mary. She is neither passive nor weak. Her active *yes* allows God to do "great things" in her.

Fiat releases God's power to love. *Fiat* reveals a receptive complement to God's initiative—a woman's willingness to receive God's perfect plan and timing in all things.

Humility, I've come to learn, detaches us from what fails to satisfy. Only by getting rid of the excesses (sins, vices, etc.) that are attached to our souls can we have the empty space that God longs to fill. Then we can be empowered to do great things that bring his love and redemption to the world.

In trying to imitate Mary, I experienced a curious calculus: in saying *yes* to God and saying *yes* to loving others, I was indeed saying *yes* to me but in the least selfish and most satisfying way possible. That is, my happiness in being a woman is found in being actively responsive to others. Receptivity was a new kind of strength, allowing me to say *yes* to the woman I was designed to be. Yet I had more to learn. Blessed John Paul II's theology of the body filled in the gaps. Part of John Paul's legacy to the Catholic Church includes many writings extolling the dignity of women. His faith-filled biblical scholarship, years of pastoral work as a priest and bishop, and his love of the Blessed Virgin Mary all combined to make him uniquely suited to speak words of blessing and healing to women and men.

Theology of the body posits that our human bodies reveal something of the glory of God. With careful application of scripture and Church teaching, John Paul II offers great insights concerning the beauty of human nature:

> The body, in fact, and only the body, is capable of making visible what is invisible: the spiritual and divine. It has been created to transfer into the visible reality of the world the mystery hidden from eternity in God, and thus be a sign of it. (*General Audience*, February 20, 1980)

Very simply, our creation as male and female is not only a great blessing to us, but it also speaks a unique language of the body. That language sheds light on the meaning on the invisible God and on the deeper truths regarding our physical life, the life we live in our bodies.

We image God—the Trinity—as male and female persons. Moreover, Christ became a man born of a human mother, Mary. Jesus' taking on a human body is not a reduction of God's divinity, but a lifting up of our humanity and a deepening of our dignity:

> [Jesus] restores the divine likeness which had been disfigured from the first sin onward. Since human nature as He assumed it was not annulled, by that very fact it has been raised up to a divine dignity . . . by His incarnation the Son of God has united Himself in some fashion with every man. . . . Born of the Virgin Mary, He has truly been made one of us, like us in all things except sin. (*Gaudium et Spes*, 22)

Therefore, our bodies are sacred. Everything about our bodies matters. Nothing is inconsequential. Being a woman matters. Being a man matters. Being in relationship matters. Masculinity and femininity explain and complete each other.

Remember the Trinity being an exchange of love between divine persons? In an analogous way, marriage and family life can image the Trinity by becoming a communion of persons. The maleness and femaleness of the bodies of husband and wife fit together in an exchange of love. The sexual complementarity of a man and woman, united in the spousal embrace of sexual union, has the potential to conceive a third person, a child, completing the analogy. Of course, let it be said that God in the Blessed Trinity is pure spirit, not male or female, and far beyond the boundaries of this analogy. Yet analogies help illuminate truth for our human minds. Therefore, according to this theology of the body, the human love—spousal love—of a man and woman is capable of imaging the truth of God, as it speaks of our higher calling, that of being united to God and to a communion of persons both here and one day in heaven.

> The [spousal] meaning of the body is our call to self-giving love, which is written into our very embodiment as male and female. By becoming a gift to one another in a communion of persons, we learn to love and be loved as God loves, and so fulfill our highest destiny. We become a reflection of the very life and love of the Trinity and prepare to share in that life forever. This is true for every human person, whether married, single or a consecrated celibate, though it is lived out in different ways. (Healy, *Men and Women Are from Eden*, 24–25)

This imagery is so powerful that St. Paul described marriage using an analogy to Christ's relationship to the Church in Ephesians 5:21–35. Christ is the bridegroom, and the

Church is the bride: "'For this reason a man shall leave his father and his mother and be joined to his wife, and the two shall become one flesh.' This is a great mystery, and I mean in reference to Christ and the church" (Eph 5:31–32).

What does all this have to do with a woman's receptivity? A woman's receptivity finds its fullness in saying *yes* to love. A bride is beloved by the bridegroom who is willing to lay down his life for her, after the model of Christ.

> In God's eternal plan, woman is the one in whom the order of love in the created world of persons takes first root. The order of love belongs to the intimate life of God himself, the life of the Trinity.
>
> The Bridegroom is the one who loves. The Bride is loved: *it is she who receives love, in order to love in return.* (*Mulieris Dignitatem*, 29)

Femininity is a beautiful gift in God's eternal plan—not a detriment, curse, an inconvenience, or a liability to be overcome. My being a woman is not *less than* enough but *more than* enough. Indeed, it is something beautiful.

Receptivity is characterized by openness and availability to another person. Yet this is not limited to the roles of wives and mothers. All women have the gift of receptivity. You see it when people take root in women's hearts and flourish there.

Women display receptivity in the way they love and serve, receiving people as gifts. They breathe compassion into the world as they chastely whisper, "Come close. Let me hold you for a while." They are the ones who unashamedly draw us close when we need it most or pay attention to our new idea or take delight in us. They are the ones staying up late to talk to us. They are women of welcome, an open door, and mentors when we can't figure things out. They are the shock absorbers when life gets turbulent, the listeners who don't judge. They nurse our brokenness, our disabilities, and our ills. They are comforters and confidants, and we are better for their presence. They love deeply, and many have risen to the place of doing so unconditionally. They even receive our unbelief. They shelter our intentions and join their prayers to ours. In short, receptive women receive us as if we were Christ. Like Mary did.

Mary's love is our best example. She first received Jesus into her womb, birthed, and nursed him. She raised him and welcomed all who entered the home of the Holy Family. Welcome and hospitality are earmarks of her receptivity. Mary opened her heart to strangers, the shepherds and townsfolk who appeared at Christ's birth. She greeted the magi. She even received from Simeon the prophetic news that a sword would pierce her heart. (See Lk 2:34–35.)

During the Nazareth years, Mary worked in the home and watched Jesus grow into a man. Imagine their walks and talks between mother and son until, finally, one sad day Mary walked beside Jesus to Calvary. There the sword of agony was unsheathed as she accompanied a wounded and bleeding Jesus to the Cross. In those final excruciating moments, her receptivity was broadened and deepened in the face of sorrow: she accepted a new son in John, the beloved disciple, whom Jesus requested she call her own. "Behold, your son." It is at that moment, the Church teaches, that Mary ultimately received us all as her children. "Behold, your mother" (Jn 19:26, 27).

Even now, Mary looks into our eyes and bids us welcome. She nods and gives us her *yes*. She invites us to come alongside her to learn the power of *yes* . . . that we may know the secret of living as a saint: that in giving we receive.

Chapter 5

Making

a Gift

of Yourself

From the very beginning, woman was a gift.

In the second creation account in Genesis, woman appears on the scene as God's good idea. The first man was alone. He had no one like himself despite an enormous creation teeming with fish and wildlife. Not a single creature would be a true companion or soul mate, so God created woman from the man's rib, and man could not be happier:

> So the Lord God cast a deep sleep to fall upon the man, and he slept; then he took one of his ribs and closed up its place with flesh. And the rib that the Lord God had taken from the man he made into a woman and brought

her to the man. Then the man said: "This at last is bone of my bones and flesh of my flesh." (Gn 2:21–23)

God brought the woman to the man, and he rejoiced. At last I have found her!

The gift of woman reveals to man the truth about himself—that he, too, is made to be given to the woman as a gift. The distinctive spousal nature of their bodies revealed the giving to and receiving from each other and the call to love and serve each other.

And the rest, as they say, is history.

It is often said that God cannot be outdone in generosity. God, who created the world out of nothing, did so out of love. God, who created man and woman, did so out of love. God, who sent his only Son to redeem his children, did so out of love. "For God so loved the world that he gave his only Son" (Jn 3:16).

Generosity is a function of charity, of love. When we love, we give. St. Paul even lists generosity as a fruit of the Holy Spirit (Gal 5:22). A woman's generosity is integral to her receptive nature. Women give gifts of themselves in physical and spiritual ways to those they love and those in need. If receptivity is one of our greatest feminine gifts found in the nature of our womanhood, then generosity is the gift that empowers it.

Generosity's actions and dispositions are the ways we demonstrate the largesse and lavishness of God's love in ours. Within our vocation, making a gift of ourselves to God and our spouse has a nobility all its own, and we'll spend some time unpacking that. Yet our generosity is not limited to that vocational call, important as it is. We are called to love and serve our neighbors, whoever they may be. In many of those cases, our generosity reflects God's presence and help through our graciousness and kind care.

In terms of living a vocation, chastity is a virtue that demonstrates generosity very well. During my engagement to Bob, I was in the midst of a busy day with all my single bridesmaids. They were helping me shop and plan for the wedding, and we were busy working through the various lists.

Dresses and shoes? *Check.* Flowers? *Check.*

Church and liturgy details? *Check.* Caterer? *Check.* Music? *Check.*

Photographer? *Check.* Gifts for the wedding party? *Check.*

Gift for the groom? They paused. "Done," I said.

"Wait a minute, Pat," they pressed. "What are you giving to Bob?"

I told them, "It's all set. We've purchased the rings, and Bob has them."

"Yes, but what else?" they begged. Surely I must be getting him a special wedding gift to remind him of the wedding day. I told them, "Trust me; he's going to remember it."

Now, they really pressed me. They were dying to know what secret gift I was not telling them about.

I was probably blushing when I said, "The gift is me."

And Bob's gift to me was himself.

We had both pledged ourselves to sexual purity before marriage, and that gift of each other's virginity was the most generous and precious gift we could give on our wedding day. We had reserved it for each other, and its value would cost us everything—a true laying down of our lives for each other.

The depths of love in this life are found through self-donation, or making a sincere gift of oneself to another.

Making a gift of oneself is a central tenet in the theology of the body. Self-donating love is how we imitate the Trinity.

This gift of self is the foundation of all Jesus taught in his command to "love one another." Jesus's passion is the most sublime example of the heroic and generous character of true love, as it is poured out for the sake of others in his death on the Cross. His life and death portrays what it means to give until it hurts. The witness of Jesus profoundly illustrates the nature of sacrifice and self-donation attached to true generosity.

Our own human love is elevated by the call to love in imitation of Jesus Christ:

> Beloved, let us love one another, because love is from God; everyone who loves is born of God and knows God. Whoever does not love does not know God, for God is love. (1 Jn 4:7–8)

Tucked deep in one of the documents of Vatican II, *Gaudium et Spes*, there lies a message of generosity and self-donation that is fundamental to understanding ourselves and our giftedness. God, who designed us in his image, created us to live in such a way that our lives reflect the generous and lavish love of the Trinity, where the exchange of mutual self-donating love is offered eternally.

> This likeness reveals that man [men and women], who is the only creature on earth which God willed for itself, cannot fully find himself except through a sincere gift of himself. (*Gaudium et Spes*, 24)

This gift of ourselves follows our nature and design. It is also blessed by the graces of our Baptism. In giving of ourselves, we find ourselves.

This is exemplified most remarkably, harmoniously, and generously in the sexual act between a husband and wife. That physical communion, a self-donating love, is one of the goods of the marriage, a laying down of one's life for the spouse.

It is supremely generous.

If we were to listen to the language of the body at that moment of sexual union, we might hear, in a certain sense, a surrendering and dying to oneself, while at the same time the giving of a great gift, that is laying one's life down for the spouse. The woman opens up her body and gives herself to her husband by actively receiving him. Further, should a baby be conceived from that union, she extends that gift in the donation of her body to support the life of their child. Her body's language signs that she is a life-bearer and nurturer.

Similarly, there is a dying to oneself on the part of the man, whose virility is surrendered to his wife in the act. His strength is yielded and spent for her not just in that moment, but should a baby be conceived from that union, he extends the gift in the donation of his body to work for the support of his wife and child. His body signs that he is willing to die for her not just in that moment, but also in the future by serving her and that child.

Only when we deny the dignity of the human person and the distinctiveness of each of the sexes, do we find attitudes and points of view that lower sexual intercourse as a mere form of recreation among consenting adults—a one-night affair, or a hookup. The language of the body tells a different story, a different truth. Sexual union is an exchange of persons, and the realities of sperm and ova are the stuff of generations to come. At its most generous, sexual intercourse is a bodily pledge of a dynamic and potent reality, a union of spirits. It is a bonding of souls within the bodies intended for a lifelong commitment for the sake of lives of children to come. Anything less would be lying with the language of the body and the ways bodies and souls are made. Anything less would be not just a denial of the theology of the body, but a disingenuous denial of the person.

Making a gift of oneself to another is an essential part of human life. The "other" might be God or another human person.

Theology of the body has something to say, then, to virgins today. This also includes the single woman who is divorced or widowed. Contrary to those who conclude that the virginal life or single state is a sign of isolation or seclusion, we see a vivid call for living as a life-giving member in one's community by loving and serving others chastely and creatively. Sexual energy, yoked with chaste self-mastery, becomes a source for good works in imitation of the greatest virgins who ever walked the planet: Jesus Christ and his mother, plus numerous saints who followed in their footsteps.

Generous self-donation is the reason the celibate, consecrated love of religious sisters, brothers, and priests is such a powerful sign to us today. Their generosity consists in laying down their lives and surrendering the procreative force of their own bodies in self-donation to Christ alone. Such love becomes a blessing and a source of joy. It is fruitful, even if it is never shared in sexual intercourse. On the contrary, the love in a religious's life radiates ever outward to be selfless and self-donating to the body of Christ, that is, to the People of God. Ultimately, these women and men become signs of the joy we look forward to in heaven, where the saints dwell in full communion with God and where the desire for sexual union will pale in comparison to the union of all believers with God himself.

Such generous gifts of self-donation lie at the heart of all vocations. "We love because he first loved us" (1 Jn 4:19). In a pivotal scene from the film *The Sound of Music,* Maria, an impetuous postulant at the abbey discloses her vocational crisis to Reverend Mother. Having set her mind on becoming a nun, Maria now fears falling in love with a widower and his children. The wise Reverend Mother does not dismiss · Maria's genuine love for God, but counsels, "Maria, the love between a man and a woman is holy, too. . . . You must find out how God wants you to spend your love. . . . You have to live the life you were born to live."

"You must find out how God wants you to spend your love." It sounds like Reverend Mother understood the generosity needed in making a sincere gift of oneself to another in the eyes of God.

How do we spend our love generously? "Love God and love others" could sum up the Ten Commandments and the teaching of Christ. Generosity is always other-directed. It is always connected with lifting up others, serving, blessing, or elevating them through the sheer graciousness of giving liberally. To paraphrase Jesus, "We go the extra mile." (See Mt 5:39–41.) It is going the distance with big-hearted energy, giving with no thought of getting.

A perfect example is the poor widow Jesus sees in the Temple. Shortly before he would enter his own suffering and give everything up for the sake of the world, Jesus points out a generous woman who is giving up everything she has:

> When he looked up he saw rich people putting their gifts into the treasury; he also saw a poor widow put in two small copper coins. He said, "Truly I tell you, this poor widow has put in more than all of them; for all of them have contributed out of their abundance, but she out of

her poverty has put in all she had to live on." (Lk 21:1–4 NAB)

Scripture scholars who have studied this passage say those two coins symbolize the two sides of charity: the widow's love of God and love of others. This woman is the epitome of generosity; she gives it all away. Hers is a generosity that goes against conventional wisdom. It's a true gift of self, a total self-emptying.

Would we look at this woman today as foolish? Isn't this behavior kind of reckless or unwise? And yet, Jesus has praise for her and her generous actions. When we give to the Lord, we are to give faithfully, totally, and freely, leaving the fruitfulness to him.

One gracious word, gift, or action can leave quite a wake. Every generous act has remarkable potentiality, a ripple effect that we may not see. There are many people this side of heaven who will never know that they have participated in the largesse of God's providence through their generosity. Fortunately, in God's economy, giving without thought of a return is never for nothing. We may never know who might be ultimately blessed by our generosity. The ripple effects are often shielded from our sight. But God uses our generosity for good, to bear good fruit. Like a seed planted in the ground, generosity has a growth that is guided by God. Each time we lavish someone with something good, true, or beautiful, there's no telling how far the blessings might reach.

The Gospel tells of another woman who is accused of wasting her resources on someone else in the name of love:

> Now when Jesus was at Bethany in the house of Simon the leper, a woman came to him with an alabaster jar of very costly ointment, and she poured it on his head as he

sat at the table. But when the disciples saw it, they were angry and said, "Why this waste? For this ointment could have been sold for a large sum, and the money given to the poor."

But Jesus, aware of this, said to them, "Why do you trouble the woman? She has performed a good service for me. For you always have the poor with you, but you will not always have me. By pouring this ointment on my body she has prepared me for burial. Truly I tell you, wherever this good news is proclaimed in the whole world, what she has done will be told in remembrance of her." (Mt 26:6–13)

This is worth pondering. . . . Do we lavish love, time, and resources on others only when and where we are able? Do we use generous care in our work in the home, in the office, in the church, in the community? Are we signs of generous love overflowing? Do we err on the side of generosity rather than stinginess or miserliness? How can our love and our work be God-centric in such a way that we elevate people before things?

Once again, Mary offers a model for generosity. Mary gave God a generous response to his love with her *fiat* at the annunciation of the angel. Filled with the joy from her encounter with the Lord, her generous spirit expanded, and she hurried to share her joy. Mary traveled to the hill country to see her cousin Elizabeth in a scene the Church calls "the Visitation." Elizabeth, too, was ready to share miraculous news that the angel already had disclosed to Mary as verification that God's power can do miraculous things. Elizabeth, who suffered from a lifetime of infertility, was now carrying a child six months along. (Reread the annunciation account in Luke 1:26–37.)

It's a scenario most women might naturally gush over—two cousins in a sweet reunion, enjoying the fact that they are both pregnant at the same time!

> In those days Mary set out and went with haste to a Judean town in the hill country, where she entered the house of Zechariah and greeted Elizabeth. When Elizabeth heard Mary's greeting, the child leaped in her womb. And Elizabeth was filled with the Holy Spirit and exclaimed with a loud cry, "Blessed are you among women, and blessed is the fruit of your womb. And why has this happened to me, that the mother of my Lord comes to me? For as soon as I heard the sound of your greeting, the child in my womb leapt for joy. And blessed is she who believed that there would be a fulfillment of what was spoken to her by the Lord." (Lk 1:39–45)

In this powerful encounter, these two long-distance cousins—Mary, miraculously pregnant with the Christ Child, and the much-older Elizabeth, carrying John the Baptist in an against-the-odds pregnancy—got their first look at one another after these miracles had occurred. The younger one, Mary, took great pains, given her times and condition, to travel the distance between her home in Nazareth to the hill country in Judah. She undertook the journey to share in Elizabeth's joy—and her own—and to do what women do: take care of each other when a baby is due. There was much to prepare!

Elizabeth offered that marvelous Spirit-inspired greeting to Mary: "Blessed are you among women, and blessed is the fruit of your womb! And why has this happened to me, that the mother of my Lord comes to me?"

Elizabeth's exclamations proclaim two truths in tandem: that Jesus is the Lord and that Mary is the mother of the Lord. In the former, Elizabeth didn't guess Mary's secret; she was given spiritual knowledge of this truth that the Messiah was hidden within the womb of Mary, just as her own baby knew it and proclaimed it by his leaping movements. Then Elizabeth proclaimed the truth that Mary is the Mother of God.

Centuries later, the Church still confirms Elizabeth's words every time we pray the Hail Mary. Elizabeth first used the words that we use today to describe Mary: she is "blessed" among women. Not only is she the most graced woman of all, but she is also the happiest of all: she has made a generous gift of herself in receiving her son, Jesus.

Following Elizabeth's greeting, Mary could not keep from singing of her joy in words you may recognize:

> My soul magnifies the Lord,
> and my spirit rejoices in God my Savior,
> for he has regarded the low estate of his handmaiden.
> For behold, henceforth all generations will call me
>   blessed;
> for he who is mighty has done great things for me,
> and holy is his name. (Lk 1:46–49)

Mary's joy becomes the source of her generosity. You could say that, in visiting Elizabeth, Mary made the first missionary journey, and to be a missionary for Christ takes great generosity. Mary joyfully brought Christ to the world, and visiting the home of Zechariah, Elizabeth, and soon-to-be-born John was just the first stop. Mary not only generously shared her joy by her words, but in her deeds of loving service to Elizabeth. The Gospel says Mary stayed three months with Elizabeth.

Women recognize the "nesting" that accompanies the birth of a first child. What a boon to Elizabeth the younger Mary must have been! What a gift to welcome a vibrant and deeply spiritual woman around the house to help her prepare for her newborn! The visit was beneficial to the newly betrothed Mary, too, who soaked up the elder Elizabeth's loving mentoring and wisdom.

You can just picture it, right?

A great sisterhood filled the next three months, a kind of working retreat for these two who loved and served each other: these women shared countless conversations over the cooking and household chores as they discussed the mysteries of life together. There was also time to pray and ponder as Mary and Elizabeth worked side by side to prepare for their babies.

These were preparations for no ordinary babies, but sons who would grow to be men with a godly mission that would change the world. But first, the generous gifts of women's presence, hospitality, and sacrificial service would prepare the way for God's Son and his messenger to enter the world.

The generous gifts of women prepare the way for the greatest gift of all: Jesus.

Chapter 6

Seeing
with Your
Heart

Tears.

They are often the first things we associate with a women's sensitivity, but they don't even begin to cover it.

The sensitivity of a woman is more than her tears at weddings or crying when watching chick flicks. It is much more. By the way, there's nothing wrong with tears whenever they come. Tears both cleanse and help heal, and in general, they are important to a person's overall health. Not to be confused with emotionalism or melancholy or heart-on-your-sleeve sentimentality that tends to focus inwardly on the self, the gift of sensitivity is way bigger, deeper, and stronger.

Much like receptivity, sensitivity senses or discerns things that relate to the heart of God and the hearts of others. It is not a weakness but a beautiful inner strength in women.

Sensitivity is a profound orientation in women that makes them quick to sense, or detect, people needing love, care, or nurture. A woman's sensitivity picks up the cues or signals others give, and it makes her receptive nature ready to respond. It is easy to see the connection with a woman's receptivity. Sensitivity is also deeply attuned to a woman's maternal sensibilities (as we find out in the next chapter).

Sensitivity is both emotional and spiritual; it leads a woman to be present and ready to love and serve someone in terms of direct care and intentional prayer. A woman's sensitivity makes connections between people and thoughtfully assists those in need.

Many times I have been on the magnificent receiving end of another woman's sensitivity, most especially when it flows from women who are my family and friends. I have also experienced it through the different women's ministries in my local parish.

Some of my fondest memories from my stay-at-home mothering years in New York come from my belonging to a parish prayer group for mothers. It was a weekly group, dubbed "Mothers' Morning of Prayer," for mothers and children to visit together to pray the Rosary aloud for one another's intentions and needs. It was a strong source of spiritual support and friendship for me for many years.

In time, my husband's work necessitated a move to Massachusetts. We were not looking to move away from our longtime home, so it was a hard decision. Before we left, the mothers' group gave us a lovely sendoff, complete with a Mass, a dinner, a keepsake photo album, and parting gifts for our new home. Most important, however, was their promise of their continued prayers. Not only that, the women challenged me to start a new Rosary group in my new town if one did not exist. In time, those prayers were answered. After finding some receptive women, Mothers' Morning of Prayer was born in my new parish.

Two years later, I was diagnosed with breast cancer. Talk about tears! The physical lump in my breast was nothing compared to the silent lump that formed each day in my throat. It was often hard to talk aloud about this situation, as my young children were always around me. Yet I let the tears and fears wash my face when I was alone or with Bob, so as to minimize the impact on my children. When I was in public, at school with the children, or at church, the women who knew my circumstances helped me keep it together.

I found endearing comfort—and the rhythm of normalcy—praying the Rosary each week in the company of those women from my parish. One day, without my knowledge, someone passed around a set of Rosary beads to all the women in the group. Each woman prayed for me on those beads. Then, again, unbeknownst to me, they sent the same Rosary beads to my former prayer group in New York, where the women there did the same thing.

Shortly before my surgery for a mastectomy and reconstruction, I walked out to the mailbox to retrieve the daily mail. A box arrived addressed to me with the recognizable handwriting of a dear friend from New York. I did not even make it back into the house. Right there I had to open it. Out came the well-traveled, well-prayed Rosary, plus dozens of cards and letters from all the New Yorkers who lifted prayers to heaven for me.

I cannot tell you the blessings I experienced in those minutes. For a few moments, time stood still, worry and stress dissipated. Joy at being spiritually and emotionally cared for, mingled with invisible long-distance hugs from friends and old neighbors, flooded my heart and leaked profusely from my eyes. I just sat in the grass in the front yard, as tears poured out of me and grace poured over me.

These women and their families had been reaching out to heaven on my behalf for weeks and weeks. Then they found a tangible way to share those prayers with me through the gift of that Rosary and their written messages of hope. My kitchen soon became wallpapered in well-wishes and cards.

That was just the beginning; their spiritual concern would turn into full-fledged physical compassion and beautiful service in the days to come.

A six-week recovery followed my surgery, when I needed rest, medication, and help orchestrating the family's schedule. I had a limited range of motion and was banned from driving—a tough situation for a busy suburban mom with children who were three, six, and nine. It was not a worry for these faith-filled women from the local Rosary group. Together with my sisters and parents, they made sure meals and carpools and laundry and housework were covered. If there was a need, someone was there to fill it, almost immediately.

What a boon—a godsend—to my husband, my children, and me! Just as Mary and others walked with Jesus on the way to Calvary, my support group was with me all the way. I was not alone in carrying my cross.

Four years later, deep into my cancer survivorship, another beautiful moment came from the hearts of these same sensitive women. For my fortieth birthday, the same two groups of women threw a surprise party at a geographically central location in Connecticut. There, the two groups from Massachusetts and New York were united for one special afternoon.

I cannot thank these beautiful women enough. Through them I healed in ways that could only come from God—thanks to their hearts being sensitive to his Spirit. Not only was I touched on the occasion of my birthday—each one a milestone for a cancer survivor—but their concern for my inner life brought an additional blessing. Missing my family and friends in New York was always a small emotional cross in relocating to Massachusetts. Through the new Rosary group, I put down roots in a new town and survived a major health crisis with phenomenal support. On that birthday, looking across the room at the faces of those women was overwhelming. Through their prayer and care, the two sides of my heart—my old life and my new life—came together.

It is not lost on me that Mary and the Rosary had much to do with all of this. Over the years, part of the power of this Rosary prayer has been Mary teaching me about the sensitivity of her own immaculate heart. One of her titles is the "Queen of All Hearts." Mary has a way of making connections and bringing people together through the Rosary, not to mention doing it in such a way as to draw us closer to Jesus.

The beauty of sensitivity is that it doesn't just see the exterior of a person, but sees the person within:

> Perhaps more than men, women *acknowledge the person*, because they see persons with their hearts. They see them independently of various ideological or political systems. They see others in their greatness and limitations; they try to go out to them and *help them*. In this way the basic plan of the Creator takes flesh in the history of humanity and there is constantly revealed, in the variety of vocations, that *beauty*—not merely physical, but above

all spiritual—which God bestowed from the very beginning on all, and in a particular way on women. (*Letter to
Women*, 12)

John Paul II's observation that women *"acknowledge the
person"* because they see with their hearts and not just their
eyes is a powerful one. Sensitivity recognizes the beautiful,
hidden dignity of other people. It is home to compassion and
mercy. It moves a woman to act deliberately to right wrongs,
assist a neighbor through works of mercy, come to the aid of
the defenseless, and bring affection and love, care and compassion to people and places where none exists. And it makes
a woman beautiful.

This sensitivity is emotional in nature in that it is characterized by a woman's sensibilities and abilities to care deeply
for people and issues that affect them. A woman may cry over
something sad or disappointing that touches her heart, but
those tears often become like fuel that powers an engine . . .
they move her to do something! Sensitivity motivates women
to act charitably and generously toward another. Yet it is also
deeply spiritual in that a woman lives from the inside out,
and her sensitivity increases as her soul is moved and nurtured by the Holy Spirit.

My experience on the receiving end of sensitivity is that
sensitivity is like one of those superhero superpowers. Some
women have become very highly attuned, with a kind of
x-ray vision of the hearts around them.

When we mention that a woman has intuition, we are
talking about a kind of sensitive radar or a thoughtful sensitivity. The woman seemingly knows things that she somehow
picked up without the kind of knowledge we associate with
book learning and analytical prowess. It is an understanding
that does not need deep conscious reasoning to decide what

to do; it seems almost instinctive. Again, this is a woman's natural sensitivity at work.

I've known women over the years whose intuition was so strong it was, at times, uncannily prophetic. I've experienced this, in rare moments, when a woman was caring for me in some way. She said something out loud that was exactly what was going on in my mind or heart, even if I had not yet articulated it.

Beyond allowing a woman to see a person with her heart, a woman's sensitivity, at its best, makes her capable of being an extraordinary listener—able to hear what's not being said as well as what is expressed. Again, her sensitivity is yoked to receptivity. The more deeply she receives a person, the more she can make a sensitive and intuitive response.

All women possess sensitivity, but it must be cultivated to bring it to full fruition. As a woman's heart is formed more and more by the love of God, she grows in grace, and her senses work in godly ways. This reflects the spiritual axiom that "grace builds on nature," and it is helpful in understanding the spiritual component of a woman's sensitivity. The more a woman grows and develops a calm and quiet spirit of sensitivity, the more responsive she is to the promptings of the Holy Spirit, to the quiet voice of truth that resonates inside of her. A woman's sensitivity aids her, like holy radar, to receive what God says to her in prayer. And when she grows in the gift of prayer, God will invariably ask her to invite others to pray with her or to become an intercessor for others.

Edith Stein wrote about the feminine soul and sensitivity. She was a Jewish convert to Catholicism, a philosopher, and an educator during the twentieth century. She eventually became a Carmelite nun, taking the name Teresa Benedicta of the Cross. Tragically, her life ended with the atrocities of

World War II. She died in a gas chamber at the Auschwitz concentration camp in 1942. In 1998, Pope John Paul II canonized Teresa Benedicta. Writing many essays about women's concerns, she characterized a woman's soul as deeply sensitive yet strong, especially when closely aligned to Christ.

> The soul of woman must therefore be *expansive* and open to all human beings; it must be *quiet* so that no small weak flame will be extinguished by stormy winds; *warm* so as not to benumb fragile buds; *clear*, so that no vermin will settle in dark corners and recesses; self-*contained*, so that no invasions from without can imperil the inner life; *empty of itself*, in order that extraneous life may have room in it; finally, it is *mistress of itself* and also of its body, so that the entire person is readily at the disposal of every call. (*Essays on Women*) [Washington, DC: ICS, 1996], 132–33)

Stein's words reflect the acknowledgment of the human person. We glean the message from Stein's description of how perceptive and protective of the inner life of the other person a woman's soul must be. And we see it in the soul's readiness to respond, being anchored to a deep receptivity of another.

Sensitivity allows a woman to be a visionary who sees into situations that require a delicate or healing touch. This visionary sensitivity motivates women. They become missionaries to the troubled areas of our culture and the world. It is why we find so many women in the so-called helping professions, for this is an arena where they excel, where feminine gifts bless the world. It is also why so many women become involved in political and social causes—to elevate and acknowledge the dignity of the human person. Women see a need and move to fill it:

Many people see sensitivity as a weakness, not realizing that it is actually a strength, a gift that women have to see beyond the exterior and look into the deepest needs of the heart, never separating the inner person from his outward contribution.

This sensitivity to others can be employed in the public realm and have an incalculable influence on public policy. When one Catholic teenager took on the fashion dictates of a giant department store, the store listened to her demand for fashionable clothing that was also modest. When nurses spoke out for increasing nutrition for unresponsive patients at hospitals, hospital policies changed. In a significant number of these "hopeless" cases, the increased attention brought patients back to health.

When women lobby for more humane treatment of prisoners, laws are changed. When women fight against the sex industry's assault on community values, zoning laws change. When women fight against pornography's assault against the human person, public policy follows their lead. . . . The Church urges women to exercise their sensitivity to restore awareness of the humanity of each person. (Mary Jo Anderson, "Feminine Genius," [*This Rock Magazine*, July/August 2005], 18–21)

Sensitivity re-sensitizes the world to the beauty of humanity, to the beauty of relationships and their natural and spiritual connection to each other. A renewed and deepened sensitivity on the part of women, especially one woman to another, is, I believe, the way women will find reconciliation on the difficult flashpoints of disagreement that divide them on the so-called pelvic issues of the day (contraception, abortion, in-vitro fertilization) and the end-of-life life issues (euthanasia and right-to-die initiatives).

Women have a sublime role in the world, not only to be sensitive themselves but also to teach others the value of sensitivity toward the human person. They are called to give a beautiful witness by the sensitive ways they embrace other people so that others can follow their lead in humanizing society.

> The heart has an intuitive sense, more or less intense, that enables us to perceive the needs or sufferings that others would not notice. My own experience of life has convinced me that never a day goes by without our meeting someone in distress of body or soul, some form of sorrow or poverty, and there must surely be many more that we miss. Look around you, my friend, and you will soon see that your good heart does not need glasses. (Elizabeth Leseur, *Selected Writings* [Mahwah, NJ: Paulist Press, 2005], 205)

A sensitive woman is beautifully dignified by the way she operates and extends her sensitive nature to others. When used generously, sensitivity is another *yes* for the sake of others. A woman's sensitivity does not draw attention to itself; its value is in the gift she gives away.

The ideal model and our mirror for sensitivity is who else? Mary.

It's hard to imagine a happier event than a wedding. Sensitivity not only helps people in trouble or in need, but joyfully delights in another's happiness by entering into the joy of the moment as well. John's gospel describes the wedding at Cana as the setting where Jesus' first miracle takes place at the request of Mary, who acts in order to keep the joy flowing:

On the third day there was a wedding in Cana in Galilee, and the mother of Jesus was there. Jesus and his disciples were also invited to the wedding. When the wine ran short, the mother of Jesus said to him, "They have no wine." [And] Jesus said to her, "Woman, how does your concern affect me? My hour has not yet come." His mother said to the servers, "Do whatever he tells you."

Now there were six stone water jars there for Jewish ceremonial washings, each holding twenty to thirty gallons.

Jesus told them, "Fill the jars with water." So they filled them to the brim. Then he told them, "Draw some out now and take it to the headwaiter." So they took it. And when the headwaiter tasted the water that had become wine, without knowing where it came from (although the servers who had drawn the water knew), the headwaiter called the bridegroom and said to him, "Everyone serves good wine first, and then when people have drunk freely, an inferior one; but you have kept the good wine until now."

Jesus did this as the beginning of his signs in Cana in Galilee and so revealed his glory, and his disciples began to believe in him. (Jn 2:1–11 NAB)

Mary perceives a need and fills it. She spots a potentially embarrassing situation for her friends, the hosts at the wedding feast: "They have no wine." She moves on this need quietly and resolutely. She knows the divine power present in her son, yet she respects his autonomy.

Mary's directive to the servers also becomes good advice to women who question the sensitivity they are exercising: "Do whatever he tells you."

The ripple effect from Mary's sensitivity blesses the whole community gathered to celebrate the wedding. All present get to enjoy the fine wine that is supplied, and Jesus's disciples see and believe. Another ripple stretches all the way into the present—this foreshadows the miracle of Jesus being made present in the new wine of the new covenant, the Eucharist.

> In the busy atmosphere of a wedding feast, she [Mary] alone realized that the wine was about to run out. And to avoid the spouses' joy becoming embarrassment and awkwardness, she did not hesitate to ask Jesus for his first miracle. This is the "genius" of the woman! May Mary's thoughtful sensitivity, totally feminine and maternal, be the ideal mirror of all true femininity and motherhood! (John Paul II, *Angelus Address*, July 23, 1995, 3)

Mary makes connections. She connects people to her son and her son to people. She mediates troubles. Her counsel to "do whatever he tells you" is good advice, coming from her heart that is perfectly aligned with God's will. Here we note, again, that even the Mother of God submits, ultimately, to God's authority. Mary is sensitive to God's directives while being sensitive to the needs of those within her sphere of influence and care.

Mary's influence also takes place in a public setting. She does the right thing for the right reasons. Mary shows us that while visionary sensitivity opens us to be missionaries, sometimes the mission is in our own backyard, right where we live and work.

The late founder of the Missionaries of Charity, Mother Teresa of Calcutta, who was beatified in 2003 by Pope John Paul II, exemplified how thoughtful sensitivity is faith in action:

You can find Calcutta all over the world, if you have the eyes to see. Everywhere, wherever you go, you find people who are unwanted, unloved, uncared for, just rejected by society—completely forgotten, completely left alone. (Mary Poplin, *Finding Calcutta: What Mother Teresa Taught Me About Meaningful Work and Service* [Downers Grove, IL: InterVarsity Press, 2008], back cover)

Sensitivity in a woman is the eyes to see people with the heart. The following is a good prayer to help sharpen your vision in this area: "Jesus, break my heart with what breaks yours."

Don't be surprised if that prayer brings you to tears.

Chapter 7

Entrusting Your Maternity to Eternity

Nothing rocked my world as much as motherhood.

Nothing has brought me to my knees or made me laugh more uproariously. Nothing has confused or challenged me or given me a glimpse of God's love as being a mother.

With the arrival of her first child, a woman undergoes a titanic change, a shift in identity and responsibility from what she was or did before. She is now forever a mother and in charge of the life of her child until he or she is grown. Even after a child reaches maturity, she remains a mother in a more nuanced way.

A child is a profound and humbling gift to receive; at the same time, the child is poised to receive everything a mother can possibly give. Mothering is hard work and sacrifice, yet most women joyously bear it for love of their children.

The sacrificial side of motherhood first becomes evident during a pregnancy. A woman yields her body and well-being so that a child may take shape and develop. The process changes her shape and her calendar forever. While a biological mother conceives and gestates and gives birth, all mothers understand sacrifice as they nurture and rear their children. The shedding of blood, sweat, and tears is more than an apt proverb.

Yet, motherhood is also a life of deep joy. Mothers are routinely awed and delighted by their growing children as well as buoyed by their smiles and achievements. Often, when women lovingly gaze at their children, they are transported by belief in all that is true, good, and beautiful. And that is a very good thing. It bespeaks an encounter with the holy.

Motherhood is a call to love more deeply, unconditionally, unreservedly, and heroically—more and more like Jesus. That's the reason why motherhood is a vocation. It becomes a path to sanctity. Motherhood becomes a response to the call to holiness, not only for the mother herself, but also for all the souls within range of her care.

Before I took my first pregnancy test, I pretty much knew. The subtle queasiness quickly gave way to full-blown nausea. I was the vomit queen. No so-called pregnancy glow for me. If I was upright, chances were good that I was turning green. (Nowadays I understand there are a few more natural and medicinal interventions for this symptom of pregnancy, so I don't want to discourage any future mothers who are reading this.)

My morning sickness was not limited to the morning. It was a round the clock. Honestly, it was hard for me to see the beauty of maternity from my usual vantage point, clinging as I was to the bathroom's porcelain bowl.

I threw up day and night, at home, at the office, in the car, at the grocery store—you name it! This once-capable, take-charge woman was subject to something out of her control, surrendering to wherever it was taking her. I so wanted to serenely concentrate on loving this baby during those nine months. But there was not much serenity within my hormonal hurricane. I just needed to cope. Pregnancy brought the Christian principles of laying my life down and making a gift of myself beyond the theoretical and into a daily gut-wrenching practice. Somehow I slogged through each month, comforted that this was on behalf of someone whom I would meet face-to-face one day.

My daily prayers were reduced to small, weakened grunts heavenward: "Jesus, help me." Or, more often, "Jesus save me."

Jesus did help me. He used that opportunity to introduce me to his mother, whom I had long ignored. It was as if Jesus finally found me in a place where I was no longer preoccupied with my own agendas. My heart was finally roomy enough for a new baby, a new life, and a new friend in his mother, Mary.

You may have wondered how I made the transition from being a woman who kept her distance from Mary to being a woman who prayed the Rosary and helped found Rosary groups for mothers. Finding Mary within my not-so-beautiful moments of maternity brought about the change.

Prior to my first pregnancy, I had always gone directly to Jesus in prayer for help. But what I needed now was some spiritual girl talk; I longed for a strong feminine connection. Through that need, I became more open to looking at Mary as more than the biblical woman whose tranquil mother-and-child portrait looked back at me from inside Christmas cards. I needed nurturing and I needed it now, as my mother and sisters lived far away, and most of my peer group had yet to have children.

Fortunately, a woman I knew from church reached out to me. I'm pretty sure Jesus placed her in my life for exactly this time. She was a mother of three and a little older and wiser than I was. She gently encouraged me to look to Mary for help and example. Then she gave me a tiny book of prayers about Mary and motherhood. It brought me consolation and became my lifeline when I felt I was drowning at sea. Though I felt weak and helpless and really seasick, I began to ask Mary to pray for me and with me. It couldn't hurt and might help.

During those nine months, Mary became my friend and a powerful intercessor. I had kept Mary on a distant shelf like a lifeless statue, but over time, she became to me a living, holy presence. Much to my surprise, Mary took me in, slowly mentoring me. Me! The woman who doubted I had any real need of her.

Mary taught me a lot of faith lessons and lessons in growing a mother's heart. It wasn't pretty. Lesson one was this: there is a way through suffering by joining my little sufferings with the tremendous sufferings of Jesus. Mary had her sorrows in life, too, but her *yes* to God and to his will was not only a *yes* to the good things God had in store for her, but it was a *yes* to whatever struggles and trials might come along the way, too. By keeping her heart close to Jesus's heart, Mary would bring love to the world in any circumstance. Through Mary I learned how to offer up the rest of my pregnancy as a gift for the sake of my unborn baby and future family.

Mary taught me to love Jesus more, reminding me to "do whatever he tells [me.]" My devotion to the Rosary grew, with its meditations on the lives of Jesus and Mary. It is a prayer well suited to pondering, which is something I felt my motherly heart doing a lot more of, once the fog of morning sickness and sleep deprivation lifted.

Mary walked alongside me in that pregnancy and all the subsequent years of motherhood. Like a good friend, she's never stopped making connections between me and other people, interceding for my needs, and sharing her treasures with me. It was like she was using my experiences in motherhood to mother me as well.

I did not know it at the time, but I was being spiritually mothered by Mary and by the caring, nurturing women who came into my life in the course of those years. Yet I had no prior frame of reference for knowing about spiritual motherhood or spiritual maternity.

I would later learn that this spiritual motherhood is the deepest and most challenging calling of every woman, in imitation of Mary.

A happy coincidence occurred when my children were small. During that time, I discovered, and was encouraged by, the writings of John Paul II, a pope devoted to Mary and gifted with an intense love for supporting marriage and families. In 1988, the year after my first child was born, the pope released a document titled *Mulieris Dignitatem* (On the Dignity and Vocation of Women). In it, John Paul II taught that women, by the beauty of their physiology and God-given design, are uniquely entrusted with human persons, and this is our feminine genius:

> The moral and spiritual strength of a woman is joined to her awareness that *God entrusts the human being to her in a special way*. Of course, God entrusts every human being to each and every other human being. But this entrusting

concerns women in a special way—precisely by reason
of their femininity. . . .

A woman is strong because of her awareness of this
entrusting . . . always and in every way, even in the situations of social discrimination in which she may find herself. This awareness and this fundamental vocation speak
to women of the dignity which they receive from God
himself, and this makes them "strong" and strengthens
their vocation. (30; emphasis added)

Remember how our being blessed comes from the core
of who we are? Our dignity is rooted in how we are made.
There's no mistaking our biology. The beauty of our feminine
design prepares us for motherhood. It flows from the sublime
blessing of who we are in our creation. Our womanly bodies are wonderfully made and purposefully created with an
empty space of a womb that we carry under our heart.

Our womb, or uterus, signals that we are made for something and someone more than ourselves. It is an organ that is
made for welcoming and receiving the life of a child, generously sheltering and nurturing the child, and finally, bringing
the child to birth. Our breasts are meant to feed that child.
Everything about a woman is made to give and support life.

The gift of maternity is being a beautiful life-bearer
through motherhood. And even if a woman never gives birth,
her life is still inclined and ordered toward mothering. Maternity is an inherent gift of femininity. That means all women
have it. All women are entrusted with the call to care for the
people within their sphere of influence. Now, this broadens
our discussion of maternity considerably.

I was very much conditioned to think of maternity as
being limited to the time of a woman's life that focuses on
the physical bearing of children, a nine-month pregnancy

that begins with conception and ends with birth and lactation of a child. Yet my experience told me maternal love and care are not restricted to childbearing alone, and John Paul II confirmed this.

Therefore our conversation about the gifts of womanhood must speak of maternity in a much broader and universal way. Maternity reflects how we are made body and soul. Being feminine means we have maternal bodies and souls.

> Woman's singular relationship with human life derives from her vocation to motherhood. Opening herself to motherhood, she feels the life in her womb unfolding and growing. This indescribable experience is a privilege of mothers, but all women have in some way an intuition of it, predisposed as they are to this miraculous gift. (John Paul II, *Angelus Address*, July 16, 1995, 1)

All women are predisposed to motherhood by their design. Yet, as we know, not all women bear children. Maternity, as described here, is not limited to those who conceive and give birth to biological children. In his 2005 text, Fr. Donald Calloway, M.I.C., references John Paul II:

> 'Masculinity conceals within it the meaning of fatherhood, and femininity that of motherhood.' What this means is that written into the . . . God-given structure of what it means to an embodied human person is the notion of fruitfulness and vocation. (*Theology of the Body and the Marian Dogmas* [Stockbridge, MA: Marian Press], 49)

The structures or anatomy of our bodies reveal our vocation and the way we are called to be fruitful. Men and women find their true fulfillment in paternity and maternity, respectively.

A woman's body was made to nurture and bring life into the world. Her vocation resembles her maternal nature; it bears fruit that gives life. A woman's relationships with others, even though they may not be fruitful biologically, as in giving birth to a child, can be fruitful spiritually. Her receptivity and her generous and sensitive care of others can give birth to good fruit of a spiritual nature in the lives of other people. In this way, a woman's life-giving gift of self to others is made through loving service, bearing the good news of love through her person.

All women are predisposed to this gift of maternity, yet it will be lived in different expressions, according to her state in life. Therefore a woman's life—her feminine genius—is characterized by physical and spiritual motherhood.

Even the mother of children must attend to this spiritual mothering, according to John Paul II, lest her physical maternity suffer or be incomplete:

> And does not physical motherhood also have to be a spiritual motherhood, in order to respond to the whole truth about the human being who is a unity of body and spirit? Thus there exist many reasons for discerning in these two different paths—the two different vocations of women—a profound complementarity, and even a profound union within a person's being. (*Mulieris Dignitatem*, 21)

We are beautifully designed with feminine gifts, maternity being the most exalted. Maternity is a gift, not a curse, as some have erroneously characterized it in our society. The fall in Eden may have resulted in consequences that include a woman's pain in the process of childbirth, but it did not mar the beauty or the birth of a child itself.

When I was a child in the sixties, a pregnancy was still called "a blessed event," but as I grew older, that awe and respect was lost in the wake of the sexual revolution. Easy access to birth control and, eventually, abortion on demand redefined a woman's fertility and maternity. No longer seen as gifts by some, fertility and maternity became liabilities or threats to a woman's potential happiness or earning power. An unplanned pregnancy in marriage became a mistake, an "oops." The child of an unplanned pregnancy for a single woman became disposable via abortion if the mother and father did not want to keep the child or put it up for adoption. Maternity became a faculty to be managed, not a gift to be received.

The core of womanhood—our feminine genius, especially the maternal gift—is often ignored, criticized, rejected, or stifled. Contraception and access to abortion desensitizes many women (and men) to a woman's feminine gifts. They close our receptivity, limit our generosity, blunt our sensitivity, and sterilize our maternity. Inherent in our dignity as women is the strength to accept or reclaim our feminine genius, for our own sakes and for the sake of humanity that is ultimately entrusted to our care. This is why we've seen the growth of natural family planning (NFP) methods, and the science behind it. NFP affirms the dignity of both spouses and, most especially, the gift of a woman's fertility and maternity.

For those among us who have been hurt or who have hurt others by disrespecting their feminine gifts, there is hope. It starts by recovering our own sensitive vision in seeing into our own lives. Then, in the name of our dignity—which we can never lose—being gentle and generous with ourselves in dealing with our own failures and sin in terms of our sexuality or our maternity.

The God of love, Jesus, who came through the gift of maternity in his mother, Mary, desires to heal us of every mistake, any sin, no matter how grievous or painful. The God of love desires to see our maternal gift rightly restored spiritually, if not physically. God's restoring grace can be poured upon our human nature to bring us peace. It may seem impossible to our human minds, but God promises mercy and forgiveness—no matter how we've erred—when we turn to him.

> Seek the Lord while he may be found,
> call upon him while he is near;
> let the wicked forsake their way,
> and the unrighteous their thoughts;
> let them return to the Lord,
>   that he may have mercy on them,
> and to our God, for he will abundantly pardon.
> For my thoughts are not your thoughts,
> nor are your ways my ways, says the Lord.
> For as the heavens are higher than the earth,
> so are my ways higher than your ways
> and my thoughts than your thoughts. (Is 55:6–9)

When we understand our own sublime dignity, that each of us truly began in God's thoughts, then we can see and know that even a child conceived under the most heinous or grievous or unloving circumstances—or one that is lost to us through natural miscarriage or an intentional abortion—is still made in the image of God, destined to share in God's plan for eternity.

John Paul II's writings about the feminine genius, together with the theology of the body, opened my eyes to the real possibility of a new feminism, or at least a better integrated one, that values women in a beautiful totality that is in harmony with their created design—holistically and organically.

This beautiful view of womanhood not only exalts womanly dignity, but it does so without devaluing men or their masculine gifts. A woman's receptive nature, again, is complementary to the design of a man's generative nature. The diversity and distinctions of gender are not negatives but positives.

All life is a blessing flowing from God's good creation. Childbearing was always part of the original gift to men and women from the Father, who blessed them to be fruitful and multiply. Women were made to be mothers as part of God's good and eternal plan.

We know this truth, finally, in that the Father sent his Son into the world via Mary's maternity: "When the time had fully come, *God sent forth his Son, born of a woman* (Gal 4:4). Thus there begins *the central event, the key event in the history of salvation*" (*Mulieris Dignitatem*, 3). Mary's maternity had ramifications for eternity. What was foreshadowed after the fall would come to pass. A Savior would be given human life through Mary's womb. Now, the motherhood of every woman is understood in light of the new covenant in the Gospel. All future children of God would likewise pass through the wombs of their mothers first and then be reborn in Baptism.

> Motherhood has been introduced into the order of the Covenant that God made with humanity in Jesus Christ. Each and every time that *motherhood* is repeated in human history, it is always *related to the Covenant* which God established with the human race through the motherhood of the Mother of God. (*Mulieris Dignitatem, 19*)

Mary's child, Jesus, makes her blessed among women. The Church honors her as the Mother of God, the *Theotokos*, or God-bearer. But every woman who conceives and bears a child is, in some way, blessed, for she carries a soul destined for eternity.

Therefore, maternity is a beautiful gift linked with eternity. That's why Mary and motherhood are coupled with the Church's identity, and why the Catholic Church is called "Mother." The Church offer rebirth through the waters of Baptism, but first our earthly mothers had to give birth to us.

Mary's maternity also points to deeper Christian discipleship, where followers fall in love with Christ and commit to honoring and serving that relationship. Mary is not only Jesus's mother, but she is the first disciple to receive him. Mary first held God himself within her very person and in her hands. Her *fiat* not only gave birth to Jesus in her heart spiritually, but she fulfills it emotionally and physically, too. She was the first to gaze upon him, to hold him, to rock him, and to nurture him.

John Paul II called Mary "an unparalleled model of love which should inspire us every time we receive Eucharistic Communion." Of Mary, he wrote in *Ecclesia de Eucharistia*:

> There is a profound analogy between the *Fiat* which Mary said in reply to the angel, and the *Amen* which every believer says when receiving the body of the Lord . . . we are asked to believe that the same Jesus Christ, Son of God and Son of Mary, becomes present in his full humanity and divinity under the signs of bread and wine. . . .
>
> Mary also anticipated . . . the Church's Eucharistic faith. . . . She became in some way a "tabernacle"—the first "tabernacle" in history—in which the Son of God, still invisible to our human gaze, allowed himself to be

adored by Elizabeth, radiating his light as it were through the eyes and the voice of Mary. (55)

Mary can help us become more devoted to Christ in the Eucharist. The next time you go to Communion, think of Mary and ask for the openness to receive Jesus the way she received him. If perchance you need some healing or some help being open to your gift of maternity, try entering into that prayer at Communion in Mass. Adore Jesus in the tabernacle of your own heart as you receive him. Ask him to strengthen your maternal gift in whatever way best suits your state in life.

In the Eucharist, Christ makes a gift of himself to you in his Body and Blood: "The Eucharist is the sacrament of our Redemption. It is the Sacrament of the Bridegroom and of the Bride" (*Mulieris Dignitatem*, 26).

May our *amen* to Christ and our *amen* to motherhood not only rock the cradle but rock the world.

Conclusion to Part Two

The gifts you have are for you, but they are never for you alone. Your receptivity, generosity, sensitivity, and maternity are relational. They are gifts given to women, not only for our personal growth, but also for the sake of our relationships with God and others. They equip us to be bearers of love to the world, to extend the eternal exchange of love that we've been invited into.

We are blessed and we are beautiful and that alone would be enough to celebrate the gift of our womanhood, but there's so much more. Knowing our dignity and our gifts help us understand what's on our inside so that we can live from the inside out. These gifts are the catalysts for action. They are the equipment we need to live out our mission in life: "For the gifts and the calling of God are irrevocable" (Rom 11:29).

Part Three

THE
BODACIOUS
MISSION
OF WOMEN

The priceless gift of womanhood is celebrated in discovering or recovering our bodacious mission to be mothers—by becoming a physical mother or a spiritual mother or both—to be life-bearers in this world and in light of eternity. We do this in ways appropriate to the vocation we have in life. Our femininity—and our design and capacity to receive, conceive, and nurture the gift of life—is never checked at the door or left behind; we bring it to everything we say and do. God's

plan for us includes our being women who live our femininity to it fullest potential.

It is a bodacious experience to meet and know a woman
who lives the fullness of her being blessed and beautiful. This
is what this book is aiming for. Be that woman!

Chapter 8

Raising
Saints
for Heaven

"This is my body, which is given for you" (Lk 22:19).

These words of Jesus captured the heart of his mission. His life on earth would be given in sacrifice on the Cross for the sake of our redemption from the sins that separated us from God. For Catholics, these precious words also capture the institution of the Eucharist, the great sacrifice and sacrament considered to be the source and summit of their faith.

In these holy words, uttered in prayer by a priest at Mass, we cannot escape the "bodiliness" of God—the truly superlative way that Jesus continues to be present in the world today—that his flesh and blood would be miraculously concealed under the auspices of consecrated bread and wine that we consume in the Eucharist.

"This is my body, which is given for you."

These words reveal the significant value and sacredness of our own bodies. And if you'll forgive the informality, the bod that God created for us is bodacious! Everything God does, he does for a reason. Our bodies have as much meaning in the eyes of God as our souls, to which they are remarkably joined.

Dictionaries list meanings for the word *bodacious* as "most excellent" or "remarkable" or "audacious in a way that is considered admirable." Some consider the word *bodacious* a portmanteau, a word that is a linguistic blend of two meanings, such as "bold" and "audacious." How *bold* that our God would come to earth as a human person in a body, and how *audacious* that our bodies might somehow image the divine God who made us and one day be glorified in heaven!

Our Creator creates the body; our Baptism consecrates the body. Through Baptism, the body is baptized and anointed, as the soul is marked with the sign of faith. A woman's body is part of the Body of Christ. So, too, is a man's body. We are grafted in our entirety into the Body of Christ.

Just as the body of Jesus exemplified his mission as the Christ, so, too, the mission of the Christian is lived in and through the body. We do all things—we carry out our mission—in our bodies and through our bodies. Indeed, our bodies belong to the Body of Christ.

Catholic churches have depictions of the body of Christ on the crucifix—Jesus' broken body hanging on a cross. We are confronted with the bodiliness of God. In his suffering and broken body, we can see our own wounds of body and soul. Through our sin and ignorance, we defile the body, revile the body, ignore the body, and denigrate the body. Yet in the crucifix, we also are confronted with the godliness of grace. Through Christ's sacrifice, the deepest graces are found in the Body of Christ—graces to restore and heal the brokenness we find in ourselves.

"This is my body, which is given for you."

The body of a woman signifies her mission; she is designed to mother.

Our female bodies point to the bodacious, life-giving mission of women. The mission of the eye is to see. The mission of the tongue is to speak. The mission of the skin is to feel and protect. The mission of the uterus is to house new life. The mission of the breast is to nourish.

"This is my body, which is given for you."

With all due reverence, these could be the same words that a mother might say to a child growing in her womb. A pregnancy is a concrete way to lay one's life and body down for another person. (Now imagine the reality of the mother of multiples carrying more than one baby!) Recall the generosity and beauty of mutual self-giving, self-donating love between spouses. In pregnancy, a woman builds on this self-donating love. She makes a minute-by-minute gift of self to her unborn child.

I've mentioned my own pregnancy struggles. My third trimesters for my three pregnancies were as unpredictable as my first trimesters and filled with medical testing. I was poked and prodded and checked for blood-pressure issues, gestational diabetes, large-gestational-age issues, and more. These, plus the returning nausea and heartburn that I began each pregnancy with, brought bouts of worry and uncertainty for me.

Yet the Christian is called to rely on God: "Cast all your anxiety on him, because he cares for you" (1 Pt 5:7). Despite my temperament's bent toward worry, I did something each

Sunday that brought me great peace: I attended Mass and received the Lord in the Eucharist.

I lived to hear those words: "This is my body, which is given for you." And I tried to join myself to the words as Christ joined himself to me through that sacrament.

As I received the nourishing host and the precious blood at the altar, I imagined the Lord's Body and Blood pumping through my veins, reaching through the umbilical cord where my unborn baby received nourishment. My heart was consoled that my baby "received" Christ in some miraculous way that was unknown to me from a scientific or biological standpoint, but in some kind of supernatural way, very much known to Jesus. As I was being touched by and nourished by Christ, so was my child. And with each Communion, I made a deeper connection with the baby that was yet to be born.

Philosopher Alice von Hildebrand captures the immense privilege women have as they participate in the biological and spiritual processes of maternity. In *The Privilege of Being a Woman*, she explains the following:

> The special role granted to women in procreation . . . is highlighted by the fact that as soon as she has conceived (and conception takes place hours after the marital embrace), God creates the soul of the new child *in her body*. This implies a direct "contact" between Him and the mother-to-be, a contact in which the father plays no role whatever. This contact gives the female body a note of sacredness, for any closeness between God and one of His creatures is stamped by His Holy Seal. This divine "touch" is . . . a special female privilege that every pregnant woman should gratefully acknowledge. (Naples, FL: Sapientia Press [2007, 6th edition], 86)

While pregnant, a woman has the unique privilege of carrying two souls in her body: hers and her child's. My sense of this was magnified every time I received the Eucharist during pregnancy. Before I ever got to teach my children about Jesus or the faith, God had already visited my womb in creating the souls of my sons and daughter and "touched" them in their creation and via the Eucharistic miracle. This armed me with confidence that I was never alone in caring for this tiny child in utero. It also indicated my growth as a spiritual mother, as praying for this child was a totally natural thing to do. Spiritual mothering was something I did not have the words for when I was young, though I was slowly intuiting the reality that physical and spiritual mothering was the way my body and soul were designed.

As a parent, my spiritual maternity was found in this longing in my heart that my children might know and receive the Lord and live his will. With each successive pregnancy, this desire grew, and it motivated me to act in ways that would teach and lead my children to know Christ.

> Motherhood involves a special communion with the mystery of life, as it develops in the woman's womb. The mother is filled with wonder at this mystery of life, and "understands" with unique intuition what is happening inside her. In the light of the "beginning," the mother accepts and loves as a person the child she is carrying in her womb. This unique contact with the new human being developing within her gives rise to an attitude towards human beings—not only towards her own child, but every human being—which profoundly marks the woman's personality. (*Mulieris Dignitatem*, 18)

"This is my body, which is given for you."

This can also be the prayer of spouses as they enter into the intimacy of the marital embrace. A woman's design, like a man's design, points to complementarity. Yet that one-flesh union of being given to one another, beautiful as it is, reflects something bigger and grander than the unity of the two. Most profound is the creative capacity women and men to share in procreation; they image God the Creator through their fruitful love. Together they become cocreators with God in bringing forth a new life. And while the gifts of femininity and masculinity serve one another to create a new life, it is maternity that shelters and nurtures that life:

> Human parenthood is something shared by both the man and the woman . . . *the woman's motherhood consti-tutes a special "part" in this shared parenthood*, and the most demanding part. Parenthood—even though it belongs to both—is realized much more fully in the woman, espe-cially in the prenatal period. It is the woman who "pays" directly for this shared generation, which literally absorbs the energies of her body and soul. It is therefore necessary that *the man* be fully aware that in their shared parent-hood he owes *a special debt to the woman*. No program of "equal rights" between women and men is valid unless it takes this fact fully into account. (*Mulieris Dignitatem*, 18)

I agree that the harder part of becoming a parent remains with the childbearing that is a woman's biological role. Rather than seeing that difference as potentially a discriminatory difference, we ought to see it as a sublime dignity—that women are preciously accountable as guardians of life—and we should work toward making respect for that dignity of human life a reality in the culture we live in:

The maternal mission is also the basis of a particular
responsibility. The mother is appointed guardian of life.
It is her task to accept it with care, encouraging the human
being's first dialogue with the world, which is carried out
precisely in the symbiosis with the mother's body. It is
here that the history of every human being begins ... with
an exclusive and unmistakable plan of life. (John Paul II,
Angelus Address, July 16, 1995, 2)

My mission as a guardian of life grew in my esteem when
I fully understood it as a gift of my maternity on two levels.
First, maternity is a universal gift imparted to women with
the innate dignity and beauty of their creation. Women are
not burdened with childbearing as much as they are gifted
with childbearing. Second, it is also a unique gift when sperm
and ova meet and a particular human zygote implants into a
mother's womb. The depth of that unique gift immediately
comes to the fore whenever I talk to a woman burdened by
infertility or one who laments childlessness due to other reasons. These women, too, possess the gift of maternity, being
predisposed to its potentiality in their creation, yet a myriad
of circumstances may thwart the biological reality of having
a child of their own.

Nothing in my professional resume could have ever
prepared me for becoming a mother, except maybe the long
hours I sometimes worked. But from the very beginning, I
had the sense that I was on a mission. Physical mothering is
not limited to the prenatal months and the birth and breast-
feeding experience. Raising children requires the hands-on
work of a mother's love and physical engagement. It also
extends to all the future feeding, raising, and educating of
the child. Physical motherhood requires vision and verve,
patience and prayer, and a commitment to putting another's

needs ahead of one's own on a regular, ongoing basis until the little ones begin to do more for themselves over time.

Every mother of a family is a physical mother. While some family circumstances may not have led to a mother's birthing of her children, she is still ordered to motherhood in her blessed design. Mothering is a physical assignment, a tangible and bodacious vocation that honors God and the dignity of the human persons in her care.

Motherhood from the outside might look messy and busy and challenging and complicated, but living it from the inside out brings many rewards—not always immediate, but in the long term—through the blessing of Baptism and ongoing life with God. The paradox of parenting that I've found is that it is intensely joyous as it breaks your heart, while it completely saves your heart by breaking it open wider still, challenging you to love even more. "It bears all things, believes all things, hopes all things, endures all things. Love never ends" (1 Cor 13:7–8).

We've already touched on the blessing of Baptism. When we bring our children to the church for baptism, we bring them to Christ. We bring them to receive the grace to initiate a relationship with Christ, and through him, with the Blessed Trinity. Witnessing our children's Baptisms reminds us that parenting is not all about just maintaining their physical needs but seeing to their spiritual needs as well. This means we will have to help our children grow in communion with Christ and with one another.

This is a bodacious mission: to raise saints for heaven. Physical motherhood affords the privilege of training true disciples and future saints. In the best of circumstances, Christian mothers, in partnership with fathers, make their home a holy place, or as Vatican II taught, a "domestic church."

Finally, Christian spouses . . . in Matrimony . . . signify
and partake of the mystery of that unity and fruitful love
which exists between Christ and His Church. . . .
    They have their own special gift among the people of
God. From . . . wedlock . . . comes the family, in which new
citizens . . . are born, who . . . in baptism are made children of God, thus perpetuating the people of God. . . . The
family is, so to speak, the domestic church. In it parents
should . . . be the first preachers of the faith to their children; they should encourage them in the vocation which
is proper to each of them. (*Lumen Gentium*, 11)

One thought about the raising of saints: it helps if it is
a desire of your own heart to be a saint. Recall your own
Baptism, your heavenly destiny. When you accept the blessing of your own Baptism, you'll find that the raising of the
children you have now, or may have in the future, will call
you forward and higher in your own faith and remind you
of your own need for grace. As you love and serve more
and more, you'll yearn to provide a better example for them.
If your children are already raised when you come into a
deeper relationship with Christ, you can become a champion
of prayer and a spiritual mother for your adult children and
your children's children.

We can't give what we don't have, so the onus is on us as
parents to grow in holiness and to foster and integrate a way
of life that reflects the values of our faith. For myself, once my
responsibilities included raising children, I read more deeply
about the teachings of the Church, or at least as much as I
was reading the parenting books, and filling the gaps in my
knowledge of both.

The ways we parent, in words and deeds, should come
from the relationship that we enjoy with Christ. To that end,

the basics of conscience formation that we talked about earlier come into play in the lives of our children. So, think of it this way: the better you strengthen your relationship with God and with your spouse, the better you will strengthen the relationships with your children and the deeper you will form their conscience in knowing God and the law of love.

> What a mother ought to do . . . is to foster her children's moral development, to discover their unique personalities, and to awaken in them their highest aspirations. . . . She can gradually give them a sense of strength and serenity that is not easily disturbed, and thus she becomes a second conscience for them. When a mother has the good fortune of being able to pass on to her children the effects of her own interior experiences, she has the duty to do so. (Leseur, *Selected Writings*, 205)

Thankfully, the Christian virtues of faith, hope, and love are given to us in Baptism because grace builds on our nature. As we stay faithful to Christ in our vocation to motherhood, we can count on grace to renew and strengthen us year by year.

Some time ago in my journey as a mother, I discovered the poetic words of Cardinal Joseph Mindszenty (1892–1975) of Hungary. (For years, a greeting card containing this strong reminder of the dignity of motherhood has been taped inside one of my kitchen cabinets.)

> The most important person on earth
> is a Mother.
> She cannot claim the honor
> of having built Notre Dame Cathedral.
> She need not.

She has built something more magnificent
than any cathedral—
A dwelling for an immortal soul,
the tiny perfection of her baby's body.
The angels have not been blessed with such a grace.
They cannot share in God's creative miracle
to bring new souls to heaven.
Only a human mother can.
Mothers are closer to God the creator
than any other creature.
God joins forces with mothers
in performing this act of creation.
What on God's good earth is more glorious than this:
to be a mother?

"God joins forces with mothers." That about sums it up. If motherhood is your mission, it's great to know you have God on your side. Motherhood is God's good idea. It is part of our blessed dignity and what makes women beautiful. It is one bodacious mission!

The most important person on the earth may be a mother, but the most important mother on earth is Mary. As foretold in scripture, she is the virgin who would give birth to the newborn Savior King. Yet Mary never claimed any title for herself, other than calling herself a lowly handmaid. Her openness to God's will elected her to "the supreme office of and dignity of the Mother of the Son of God" (*Redemptoris Mater*, 39).

The key to understanding Mary is this: We do not start with Mary.

We start with Christ, the Son of the Living God! The less we think of Him, the less we think of her; the more we think of Him, the more we think of her; the more we adore his Divinity, the more we venerate her Motherhood; the less we adore His Divinity, the less reason we have for respecting her . . .

It is on account of Our Divine Lord that Mary receives special attention, and not on account of herself . . . It is her Son who makes her motherhood different.

A Catholic boy from a parochial school was telling a university professor who lived next door about the Blessed Mother. The professor scoffed at the boy, saying: "But there is no difference between her and my mother." The boy answered: "That's what you say, but there's a heck of a lot of difference between the sons." (Fulton J. Sheen, *The World's First Love: Mary, Mother of God* [Ignatius Press, 1996], 64)

That's right. We always start with Jesus when it comes to Mary. Recalling that everything starts with the exchange of love in the Trinity, we find Mary as central to God's good plan of salvation. Through her *yes* to God, Mary offered her life to bear the Son of God, who would come through her. "This is my body, which is given up for you."

In the Eucharist there is Jesus' Body and Blood taken from the body and blood of the Blessed Virgin. . . . If Adam could call Eve when she had been taken from his rib, "bone of my bone and flesh of my flesh" (Gn 2:23), cannot the holy Virgin Mary even more rightly call Jesus "Flesh of my flesh and Blood of my blood"? Taken from the "intact Virgin" as says St. Thomas Aquinas, the flesh of Jesus is the maternal flesh of Mary, the blood of Jesus is the maternal blood of Mary. (Stefano Manelli, *Jesus*

Our Eucharistic Love, http://www.marystouch.com/Eucharist/ch6.htm, accessed on September 12, 2012, chapter 6)

So let us thank the Son for the gift of his body, and let us thank Mary for her physical maternity, without which the Bread of Life could not have come into the world.

Chapter 9

Beyond Fairy Godmothers

I'm not talking fairy godmothers here.

You know the ones. They are storybook or film characters waving magic wands and—*poof*—wishes granted!

Nope. We need real-life godmothers. Not to grant wishes, though that would be a delightful bonus, but to help bring our faith to birth and nurture it.

The Church assists us in understanding what spiritual motherhood is in the role godmothers play in standing up as sponsors for another person in Baptism. In theory, a godmother is chosen to assist the newly baptized Christian in his or her continued spiritual development. It is both an honor and a responsibility. In good practice, it can be a powerful support to a godchild's faith and growth. When ignored or when assumed by a spiritually immature godmother, it becomes much less.

And yet . . . our world suffers for lack of spiritual mothers. We need women who can make a difference through their own brand of maternal leadership. We need women who are encouragers, who are willing to be more than energetic cheerleaders. We need spiritual and moral mentors.

We need women who look to God first in all things and who know how to impart what they've learned. We need more downtime with uplifting women and more upbeat women who know how to get down . . . on their knees. We need *bodacious* women—spiritual mothers—willing to take on a fantastic person-to-person mission.

At the close of Vatican II, the late Pope Paul VI offered a very potent and poignant message for women. It is still relevant for us, though it is nearly a half-century old.

> And now it is to you that we address ourselves, women of all states . . . you constitute half of the immense human family . . .
>
> But the hour is coming, in fact has come, when the vocation of woman is being achieved in its fullness, the hour in which woman acquires in the world an influence, an effect and a power never hitherto achieved. That is why, at this moment when the human race is under-going so deep a transformation, women impregnated with the spirit of the Gospel can do so much to aid mankind in not falling. (*Address to Women*, December 8, 1965)

Ladies, the hour is here. An hour that depends on women drawing deeply upon their blessedness and beauty—women *impregnated* with the spirit of the Gospel—and giving birth to faith, hope, and love, to give life to the world. This mission will be engaged rather boldly and audaciously through *maternity*—a spiritual motherhood—where women impregnated with the spirit of the Gospel will humanize our culture from the inside out:

> Spiritual motherhood . . . means nurturing the emotional, moral, cultural, and spiritual life in others.
>
> All women are called to give birth—physically and/or spiritually. All women are called to be Christ-bearers, to receive divine life in the womb of their souls and bear Christ to the world. All women are called to see in Mary's spiritual motherhood a reflection of their own lives.
>
> If all women embraced the call to spiritual motherhood they would ignite a nuclear reaction that would spread the culture of life through the whole world. The feminine genius would set the whole world on fire! (Katrina Zeno, *Discovering the Feminine Genius: Every Woman's Journey* [Boston: Pauline Books and Media, 2010], 38–40)

In the last fifty years, opportunities for women have been greater than at any time in history. Yet, this has largely been a First World phenomenon where women can be found in every professional, social, religious, and political sphere. Sadly, worldwide, we still find that not all women are free, and many face gender-based discrimination. This requires dynamic moral leadership and initiatives that shine light on the dignity of women.

The Catholic Church has recognized the voices of oppressed women and others in need, applying the law of love to injustices against human dignity. Paul VI's *Address to Women* issued a renewed call to holiness, adding a very

specific feminine angle—that of being lifesavers to a world
with a darkened moral conscience:

> Our technology runs the risk of becoming inhuman.
> Reconcile men with life and above all, we beseech you,
> watch carefully over the future of our race. Hold back the
> hand of man who, in a moment of folly, might attempt to
> destroy human civilization. (December 8, 1965, 2)

No matter what milieu you find yourself in, you can look
around and see it. More than ever, the light and love and life
women bear must reconcile men and other women to the
dignity of life. For without respect for human life on earth,
there can be no respect for life eternal.

The love of mothers, therefore, is the mission of mother
Church—to give birth to disciples through physical and spiritual maternity. Can this spiritual mothering really be God's
plan for us as women? What will our answer be? I'll speak
for myself. But first, a quick Bible story review.

There's a chapter in Genesis when God calls Abraham
to bring his son Isaac up to a mountain and sacrifice him
on an altar. To a modern reader, that seems outrageous. Did
God really ask Abraham to relinquish the very child that fulfilled the covenant (Gn 12:1–3) that he had made? The son
that would bring many descendants and nations promised
through Abraham? Yes, God did. And Abraham complied
and obeyed God's request. Save, at the last moment, God
intervened before Isaac was killed by Abraham's knife.

It was a test of fidelity. Abraham passed it, and Isaac
lived. A sacrificial offering was still made that day, according to God's plan. But instead—in a foreshadowing of God's
Son, Jesus, who would one day be sacrificed on behalf of
all—God the Father himself provided the sacrifice that day

for Abraham, as Abraham spied a ram caught in a thicket by its horns. (See Gn 22:1–14.)

I am inspired by Abraham's loyalty to God and fidelity to God's plan, even when it seems beyond his own mortal comprehension. I have never lost nor sacrificed a child as Abraham was prepared to do, but for a time, I did fear losing my own life before I had finished raising my children, given my breast cancer diagnosis back in 1996. Such fears tended to come at night. I would pray in my bed, often awash in tears. Sometimes Bob would wake and hold me and pray, and sometimes I prayed alone so that he could rest.

One summer night, in between surgeries, I awoke in bed. Another panicked weepiness had gripped me. There in the dark, with no light save the silvery beam that normally streams in from the street lamp between the shades, I listened for God in the tabernacle of my soul.

In prayer, I believe that God allowed me to see my husband and my three children as he sees them—as his own beloved children on loan to me. At the time, I was thirty-six, and Bob and I had been married fourteen years. The children were nine, six, and three.

Very tenderly and reassuringly, God seemed to say, "Pat, do you believe I love you and have a perfect plan for your life?"

"Yes, Lord. I know you love me, and my husband and children remind me of it every day. I could not ask for any more love."

"Do you believe I have a perfect plan for Bob?"

"Yes, Lord. He's been so great through all this."

Then he mentioned each child by name.

"Do you believe I have a perfect plan for Bobby?"

"Yes, Lord."

"Do you believe I have a perfect plan for Katie?"

"Yes, Lord."

"And how about little Peter? Do you trust that I have a perfect plan for him?"

By now, I discerned this was more about my trusting God the Father's care of my family than being worried about what might actually happen to me.

I replied again. "Yes, Lord. I trust you have a perfect plan for Peter and for each of them."

I waited. I had relinquished it all back to God. Consciously, in those moments, I let it all go.

God had one more question.

"Pat, would it still be my perfect plan for them if you were not in it?"

I could not fathom seeing my children grow up without me; this was exactly my sole worry. In the end, I yielded my misery to God, my fear of possibly dying young without finishing the task of raising my children.

There was only one answer.

"Yes, Lord."

In that moment, I became a spiritual mother in a way I had never expected or experienced. I surrendered my greatest gifts one by one, along with my will. I was ready to love my family and pray for them for all I was worth—trusting the results to God—right up to whenever my dying day might be.

Tears came, but with them came a deep, abiding grace and peace. Whatever came next, I knew God had my best interest at heart. And theirs. He loved me and intimately knew my deepest fear—the one deeper than my own death. More importantly, I knew God loved my family and would never forsake them. Or me.

Surrendering all to God and his perfect plan rendered me a priceless lesson. It answered the question at the heart of all true conversion: Do I love God for all his goodness to me, or do I love him?

Do I love the gifts, or do I love the gift giver?

For me, that's the key to beginning to live out spiritual motherhood—that first, we are convinced of the intimate love God has for us, and then we let that love flow out to others. It is knowing God and knowing he put us in another person's life "for such a time as this" (Est 4:14). It's trusting his timing, knowing he does everything on purpose.

Spiritual motherhood allows us to lovingly serve others, not for what they can do for us or because they love us back or because they help make us feel good. It is doing it for their sakes. It is doing it for the sake of God, as if God himself personally asked it of us. Spiritual motherhood involves a willingness to suffer, be inconvenienced, be hurt, or be taken for granted—and serving anyway.

From a logical standpoint, it will never seem fair. But God's economy operates with a different scale of values, where giving with no thought of getting makes us better. It makes us more like Jesus.

> Then [Jesus] said to all, "If any man would come after me, let him deny himself and take up his cross daily and follow me. For whoever would save his life will lose it; and whoever loses his life for my sake, he will save it." (Lk 9:23–24; cf. Mt 10:38–39; Mk 8:35; Jn 12:25)

Spiritual mothering responds to the lover we cannot see but who is found in the face of our neighbor. It loves for the sake of someone and something—the truth—we hide in our hearts. So it seems crazy, at times, by the world's standards.

It is the heart of the *yes*—the *fiat*—like Mary gave to the Father, come what may. It is her open, obedient, active, joyful *yes*, despite the sword that would pierce her heart. It was the *yes* Mary mirrored every day as she raised Jesus.

It is the same *yes* that Jesus learned from his mother, a *yes* we witness in his prayer in the garden the night before he died. He begged, "Father, if thou art willing, remove this cup from me; nevertheless not my will, but thine, be done" (Lk 22:42; cf. Mk 14:36).

A spiritual mother is a *yes*. But she is neither a doormat nor someone who insinuates herself into someone's life. She is asked—or she offers—and makes gracious replies in every case. She makes room in her person, in her heart, in her life for other people because she welcomes them as God's plan for her for the short term or the long term. She trusts God and opens herself to his plans and his people. He initiates it, and she receives it. She leaves the results, or what she may come to bear, to him. In doing so, she brings forth life more abundant than she could ask for or imagine.

> Spiritual motherhood means coming alongside and investing in the lives of younger women, through formation, wisdom, support, and encouragement. This is true for the single woman, the woman who is unable to have children of her own, and the woman who is celibate. This task cannot be underestimated. It is vital for all women to be spiritually mothering and mentoring the women who walk with them. In some cultures, older women can feel as if they no longer have anything to offer. This is a great poverty, as they in fact have a whole lifetime of wisdom desperately needed by all women, and indeed the whole world. (Karen Doyle, *The Genius of Womanhood* [Boston: Pauline Books and Media, 2009], 73)

This is about becoming a woman of holy influence, being a life-giver to others. It's about finding creative ways to love the generation that's coming up behind you (and maybe your own peer group) through your feminine gifts of receptivity, generosity, sensitivity, and maternity. One friend describes it as giving others a soft place to land. It also means leaving someone better off for having spent time in your company.

This is not about women who say they're spiritual but not religious. This is about living a Christian life sacramentally yoked to your Baptism and every other sacrament you've received, in fidelity to Christ and his bride, the Church. You need them! And it means not being afraid to share your faith candidly when asked and letting your smile and actions do the talking when you're not.

For the woman with children, spiritual mothering begins with the spiritual nurturing of her children. Educating the spirit should be as natural as any other education done on their behalf. Leading together with their husbands, wives are called to see their home as a "domestic church," where faith is first preached and lived. Once those needs are met, a woman can and should open her heart and home to serve the temporal or spiritual needs of others outside of it, as she is able.

A happily married woman might also mentor the younger women within her community, in the spirit of St. Paul's letter to Titus: "Bid the older women likewise to be reverent in behavior. . . . They are to teach what is good, and so train younger women to love their husbands and children" (Ti 2:3–4). I'm deeply grateful to the women who opened their hearts and homes to me when I was single and later a young bride. Their examples made me long for, and work for, a spiritually enriched married life.

For the single woman, regardless of age or circumstance, spiritual mothering is a spirit of service. For example, it might involve mentoring another woman who is younger and less mature. Or it might be the tending and teaching of children in a variety of personal or professional settings. Additionally, a woman can exercise a deep spiritual ministry toward others by holding them close to her heart in prayer.

These suggestions are grounded in the principles of friendship. If we have friendship with Christ, it's fruitfulness spills over into service and care that is offered in the spirit of the Divine Friend. The Second Vatican Council taught that all people are called to holiness. The call to be in relationship with God is our first and most true vocation, manifested in love of neighbor. St. Thérèse of Lisieux, famous for her "little way," offers what could be the motto of spiritual mothers: "O Jesus, my Love, at last I have found my vocation. My vocation is love!" (*The Story of a Soul*, trans. John Clarke, 3rd ed. [Washington, DC: ICS Publications, 1996], 194).

Finally, there is a sublime calling to spiritual motherhood that we cannot overlook: a woman's call to consecrated religious life. As long as there have been Christians, there have been women who have lived their vocations as consecrated virgins for the love of Jesus alone. Religious life is a beautiful, bodacious call signifying, in advance, the marriage in heaven between Christ the bridegroom and the Church as bride.

The consecrated life of a religious sister is a powerful sign that union with Christ is possible here on earth, foreshadowing the promised union with him in heaven. It's living with the end in mind, as far as humanly possible.

> Spiritual motherhood takes on many different forms. In the life of consecrated women, for example . . . it can express itself as concern for people, especially the most needy: the sick, the handicapped, the abandoned, orphans, the elderly, children, young people, the

imprisoned and, in general, people on the edges of society. *In this way a consecrated woman finds her Spouse,* different and the same in each and every person, according to his very words: "As you did it to one of the least of these my brethren, you did it to me" (Mt 25:40). . . .

This is . . . a . . . *convergence between the virginity* of the unmarried woman and *the motherhood* of the married woman. . . . A woman is "married" either through the sacrament of marriage or spiritually through marriage to Christ. *In both cases marriage* signifies the "sincere gift of the person" of the bride to the groom. In this way, one can say that the profile of marriage is found spiritually in virginity. (*Mulieris Dignitatem,* 21)

I am in awe of the many religious sisters I know and their full-on non-stop love for Jesus, their holy spouse. Their undivided hearts, in their union with Christ, give birth to spiritual "children" of all ages who are fed, housed, clothed, rescued, redeemed, nurtured, educated, and restored through the sisters' offerings of prayer and works of mercy. While a religious life has a rule of life that is scheduled and disciplined, the charism of the order determines the kind of work a sister does.

For those of us outside of religious orders, we might look at ways to be disciplined about our own prayer and work and be mindful of ways that we can be effective in our prayers and service to others.

Here are five recommendations for aspiring spiritual mothers. I share these based on my own experiences and what I've observed in others. I'm limiting my focus here to spiritual motherhood among women, for the moment, as it is often the easiest place to start.

1. *Make friends with one another.* We need to create a non-competitive sisterhood that lifts the hearts and minds of women to Christ and supports others prayerfully and charitably. We must celebrate one another's successes and be willing to stand in the mud next to one another when life is raining hard on us.

2. *Find three.* To be socially well-rounded, every woman should try to befriend at least three women: a woman who is older than herself, a woman who is younger, and at least one from her peer group. These women should be people whom she might learn from, and share her faith with, even if those friends are not exactly involved in their faith or a church. Intergenerational conversations bring learning and fun to all sides. Stumped on how to do this friend thing? Ask Mary to make a connection.

3. *Raise the fun quotient.* Joy is contagious. Be a joy catalyst for everyone around you, or die of laughter in the attempt. Your mileage may vary, but remember: "A cheerful heart is good medicine, but a downcast spirit dries up the bones" (Prv 17:22). Do things that bring a smile or joy to the woman you want to befriend. This means paying attention to what delights her, and acting on it.

4. *Pray with one another.* This is a tough one for many people. Remember, we're talking about spiritual motherhood here. Spiritual necessities cover words and deeds of lives. Therefore, we ask, seek, and knock and give our lives more and more to Christ through prayer. (See Mt 7:7.)

   Use these key words to remember how to pray with another person: ask, seek, knock. Here's how: always ask first: "Would you like us to pray about this now?" If your friend affirms, continue. If not, offer to pray for her when you pray privately or when you go to church this week. If she would like to pray, then move on to seek. Silently seek the Holy Spirit's guidance to be with you as you draw in a breath. Then knock, like you're politely knocking on heaven's door. This is where you actually pray out loud with your friend. Keep it simple: "We'll just bless ourselves, then I'll mention the need (or prayer intention) out loud, and then we can pray an Our Father and a Hail Mary."

Have faith. The more you do this, the better and easier it gets. Make this a habit with your friends, either formally or informally.

5. *Use the four gifts of receptivity, generosity, sensitivity and maternity.*

- *Be receptive.* Ask what's on your friend's heart. Then listen. Give her permission to speak without having to share your stuff. Give her undivided attention. Focus and follow up on things, even if you have to put a note in your calendar to remind you to do it. Add the following sentences to your vocabulary: "I really like that about you." "You are beautiful." "Thank you for being thoughtful." "Is there some way I can help?" "Tell me what made you happy today." "Tell me what was hard about that." "Come for dinner." "What would you like me to pray for?" "I forgive you." "I love you."

- *Be generous.* Give, with no thought of return. Pay it forward. If your friend needs something, give out of your pocket if your means allow. Ask if you can enlist others to help if there are huge needs; then do it. Do something that requires extra effort: say an extra Rosary for her or go to Mass for her intentions. Share what you know: offer to teach a skill or mentor in a competency you have. Sure, drop off dinner when she or her family is in need. She will love it, whether you cooked the meal yourself or picked it up from that nice Italian place on the corner. Bring her to church. Find your prayer style and pray every day. St. Louis de Montfort says that to be perfect, pray a Rosary a day.

- *Be sensitive.* Commit: Be there when you say you will. Don't bash, trash, or insult your friend's husband, boyfriend, children, parents, boss, friends— even if she does. Call first. A personal note trumps a text or e-mail every time. Have integrity in your work, "Whatever your task, work heartily, as serving the Lord"(Col 3:23). Speak honestly when asked about something difficult and respond with twice the love you'd normally show. Whenever you think she looks like she needs some help, that's your cue. Help. If a disagreement or a misunderstanding is older than a month and you haven't dealt with it, just let it go. Surprise her, "just because!" When in doubt, bring chocolate.

- *Be maternal.* Give life. Smile, soothe hurts, encourage. Cheer for every pregnancy and grieve every loss, and remember dates that are important in your friend's life. Nourish guests with food within your means, but let your welcome be extravagant. Invite others into your life. Offer to mind the children and give a young mother a day off or a night out with her husband. Call that single mother you know, and don't let her off the phone till you have a date to help her get that project done.

Remember, you don't have to be a therapist. Good friends can help, but deep wounds often need friendship plus professional care. Help her find a counselor or a confessor. Often she needs both.

Be the one who gently recommends the sacraments. Be that friend who is willing to bring a frightened friend back to the Sacrament of Reconciliation. Tell her you will even go with her and pray outside the confessional the whole time she is inside. And then never ask her the details. Be trustworthy.

Be affectionate within the boundaries of comfort and propriety, not only for yourself but also for the other person's sake. Keep their sensibilities and needs in mind. There's a range when it comes to physical affection, and it varies by culture, ethnicity, upbringing, and professional and personal needs for space. It's okay to ask if her if she wants a hug, or needs a good cry.

When your friend is suffering, do what you can to stay open and empathetic. Let your attitude reflect maternal stability: I will stay. I will cry with you, or I will hold your hand even when you can't explain it. We will get you through this, together. I will not stop praying for you. You are not alone. Then keep your word.

Make a prayer list. Or several.

Ultimately, spiritual motherhood is a call to pray for those within our sphere of influence, for those we hold close in our hearts. This is also, quite specifically, a call to pray for priests. A recent document from the Congregation for the Clergy in the Vatican asked women of every state in life to spiritually "adopt" a priest (or more than one) by name in prayer. It specifically recommends that we intensely pray for priests when we are praying and adoring Jesus in the Blessed Sacrament, just as Mary prayed for son as he offered his sacrifice on the Cross. For more details on this specific kind of prayer, and real-life examples of women who took this mission of spiritual maternity on behalf of priests to heart, look for the document *Eucharistic Adoration for the Sanctification of Priests and Spiritual Maternity* in the suggested readings for this chapter.

Do you need a godmother? You've already got one. She's not sprinkling fairy dust or working with a magic wand. In fact, you can probably guess that I've been leading up to this all along. Just offer up a prayer, and she's there. Of course, it's Mary. "Jesus is Mary's only son, but her spiritual motherhood extends to all . . . he came to save" (CCC, 501).

The Catholic Church teaches that Mary's spiritual motherhood began at the Cross, at Jesus's loving command. We find this scene between Jesus, Mary, and John, the beloved disciple, author of the Fourth Gospel:

> When Jesus saw his mother, and the disciple whom he loved standing near, he said to his mother, "Woman, behold, your son!" Then he said to the disciple, "Behold, your mother!" And from that hour the disciple took her to his home. (Jn 19:26–27)

Mary was the last gift Jesus made from the Cross, alongside our redemption. With his dying breaths, he put his mother in the care of one of his best friends. He gave his mother to a "son" who would revere and cherish her. For centuries, the Church has interpreted these words as more than a personal conversation between the persons there. This is the God-Man having a universal conversation with all of us. Jesus asks that we take Mary as our mother and make room for her in our homes (our lives), and he expands Mary's role to take us in as her spiritual children. "Mary united to her Son in the offering of the sacrifice, extended her motherhood under the Cross to all men and women, and in particular to the disciples of Jesus" (Benedict XVI, *Homily*, November, 29, 2006).

Pope Benedict XVI expresses deep sentiments about Mary's ever-present nearness to us. Her heavenly reign does not separate her from us, but it draws her even closer than we might think:

> Mary is taken up body and soul into the glory of Heaven, and with God and in God she is Queen of Heaven and earth. And is she really so remote from us?
>
> The contrary is true. Precisely because she is with God and in God, she is very close to each one of us.
>
> While she lived on this earth she could only be close to a few people. Being in God, who is close to us, actually, "within" all of us, Mary shares in this closeness of God. Being in God and with God, she is close to each one of us, knows our hearts, can hear our prayers, can help us with her motherly kindness and has been given to us, as the Lord said, precisely as a "mother" to whom we can turn at every moment.
>
> She always listens to us, she is always close to us, and being Mother of the Son, participates in the power of the Son and in his goodness. We can always entrust the whole of our lives to this Mother, who is not far from any one of us. (*Homily*, August 15, 2005)

Why would anyone wish for a fairy godmother? We've got God's mother as our spiritual mother! It doesn't get any richer than that.

Chapter 10

Our
Bodacious
Calling

Behold, you are beautiful, my love,
behold, you are beautiful! (Sg 4:1)

No woman can read the Song of Songs in the Bible without
being moved by its poetry that sings of the beauty of human
love, a love that climaxes in marriage and, allegorically, drips
of God's love for us. The Catholic Church, with her saints and
mystics, sees this allegory portraying the love story between
God and us. The God of love, indeed, comes in search of us,
longing that we might choose to receive his invitation of love.

I began this book sharing my love of music and song with
you. And if I could have sung this book to you, it would have

been full of vibrant and rich harmonies blended from many voices singing as one. But since this is a book, made of pages and ink, instead I went in search of the lyrics that would sing to a woman's soul from the heart of the Church itself—in the words of scripture and prayer, in church teachings and homilies, in the wisdom of saints and would-be saints, and from women themselves.

Our dignity forms the basic notes of the melody line in a woman's song. Our gifts add layers of complexity with their bright and brave chords, and our mission builds to a far-reaching dynamic crescendo that invites others to sing along.

As so, this last conversation will be a final refrain.

Your womanhood is a gift—worthy of celebrating, cherishing, and protecting.

Femininity in its fullness, naturally and supernaturally, in body and soul, is a gift from God to you to bring you into a relationship with him and with other people. It is God's plan for you. Here are a few lines that celebrate that truth:

God,
infinitely perfect
and blessed in himself,
in a plan of sheer goodness
freely created
you
to make you share
in his own blessed life.

For this reason,
at every time and in every place,
God draws close to you.
He calls you to seek him,
to know him,

to love him
with all your strength.

He calls together all of us,
scattered and divided by sin,
into the unity of his family,
the Church.

To accomplish this,
when the fullness of time had come,
God sent his Son
as Redeemer and Savior.

In his Son and through him,
he invites you to become,
in the Holy Spirit,
his adopted children
and thus heirs
of his blessed life.
(Excerpted and adapted from *CCC*, 1)

That's the plan in six carefully constructed sentences. Everything about our dignity leads us toward that blessed life. God, who is blessed in himself and has no need of anyone else, does not remain alone and isolated. Instead God opens himself to us. He freely creates us and redeems us that we might inherit blessedness.

This is the God who is crazy about us! The prophet Zephaniah gives us a vision of this Lord and God who loves us so much that he sings and rejoices over us. Ever sing a lullaby over a baby as you wept with joy for love of her? Ever sing to the man you love or dedicate a song to him on the radio or dance to that wedding song? Ever set a song on repeat in your music library because it reminds you of a dear friend?

Yeah, it's kind of like that. Only it's God, so it's an order of magnitude that is off the charts.

Even if I crank the speakers up to "stun," I'll still not hear or fathom how deep and wide and huge this love is.

> Sing aloud, O daughter of Zion; shout, O Israel!
> Rejoice and exult with all your heart, O daughter of
> Jerusalem! . . .
> The LORD, your God, is in your midst, a warrior
> who gives victory;
> he will rejoice over you with gladness, he will renew
> you in his love;
> he will exult over you with loud singing as on a day
> of festival. (Zep 3:14, 17–18)

God sings his song of love over us, and it is a celebratory festival song. I hope you've heard his singing within these pages.

Now, God invites us to return his melody.

Elisabeth Leseur (1866–1914) heard the song and lived her life in tune with it. She was a married French laywoman, and members of the Church are taking up her cause to declare her a saint. She gives us something lyrical to ponder:

> Let us love. Let our lives be a perpetual song of love for
> God first of all, and for all human beings who suffer, love
> and mourn. Let deep joy live in us. Let us be like the lark,
> enemy of the night, who always announces the dawn and
> awakens in each creature the love of light and life. Let us
> awaken others to the spiritual life. (*Selected Writings*, xiv)

The figure of the singing lark at dawn stirs me. I have often been the first one up in my household and found myself outdoors, walking my dog in the first light of dawn to sounds of twittering birds. I watch stars fade as the sun comes into view. It's a time of transition and change and awakening.

Let me make two quick points about this bird and the dawn as they relate to Mary. First, St. John of the Cross, a great spiritual director and mystic from the sixteenth century, ponders the solitary bird whose five characteristics reflect a contemplative spiritual life:

> The traits of the solitary bird are five: first, it seeks the highest place; second, it withstands no company; third, it holds its beak in the air; fourth, it has no definite color; fifth, it sings sweetly. ("The Sayings of Light and Love" found in *The Collected Works of St. John of the Cross* [Washington, DC: ICS Publications, 1991], 121)

For our purposes, let's focus on that fifth trait, that of the solitary bird singing sweetly. This describes the soul that celebrates and praises its Creator. It reflects Mary's soul as she sweetly sings her *Magnificat*: "My soul magnifies the Lord, and my spirit rejoices in God my Savior"(Lk 1:46–47). Mary, too, is a solitary bird, one-of-a-kind, the highest creature, the zenith of creation.

The Church has many titles for Mary, including the "Morning Star." Mary is the dawn of salvation, the morning star twinkling and awaiting Christ—the sun rising. For centuries, she has been a guiding light leading people home to Christ. Seafarers call her "*Stella Maris*," the Star of the Sea. Her light and her radiance bring people to Jesus.

In the new millennium, Popes John Paul II and Benedict XVI have invoked Mary as the "Star of the New Evangelization." The new evangelization is not a new gospel because "Jesus Christ is the same yesterday and today and for ever" (Heb 13:8). It is rather, a new approach to bringing others into relationship with Jesus and his Church. That's why Mary is its star. This is something she does very well.

Mary awakens in us the love of light and life. *"The Church sees in Mary the highest expression of the 'feminine genius' and she finds in her a source of constant inspiration"* (John Paul II, *Letter to Women*, 1995, 10).

Mary awakens the spiritual life in us—especially that we are blessed by the gift of our womanhood! Mary not only helps us celebrate femininity, but she also points the way toward cherishing it.

We've had several conversations related to our bodies and the meaning of our sexuality in light of our dignity and gifts. Yet, for some women, these conversations may have been difficult. Many of us have body issues needing realignment from the inside out. We must heal from the sexual hurts we have endured or from the bombardment of hedonistic cultural norms.

In discovering the beauty of my feminine gifts, I caught a new vision that freed me to be myself. In the words of St. Francis de Sales, "Be what you are, and be that well." But as you saw from my own life, things take time. Rare is the person whose conversion or change for the better is instantaneous. Despite our beautiful potentiality, we can still feel that our spiritual and personal growth is hindered by things in our past or by an enormous lack of confidence. You may feel that your own life cannot possibly measure up to some of the things we've talked about. All I can say is that God saw this day, too. He saw that you and I would struggle with the pains and shortcomings and hurts in our lives. If your conscience is making you feel like your personal sins have piled up or some other issues have stolen your ability to cherish your femininity, let me offer some advice.

First, welcome to the club. We're all sinners. That's why Jesus came. Period. Reread the plan. God's plan is for our goodness—that we might become his children and heiresses to his blessed life. I have my own foibles, and yet I very much cling to the idea that this life requires my ongoing conversion.

Second, Jesus is in the forgiveness business. He wants us to share his blessed life, and so does his Church. Memorize this: "There is no offense, however serious, that the Church cannot forgive" (CCC, 982).

Go to confession. The sacrament of Reconciliation is powerful. Make this your new resolution if it has been a while since your last confession. Until you can get there, talk to Jesus. Here's a prayer from the psalms to prepare: "Create in me a clean heart, O God, and put a new and right spirit within me" (Ps 51:10).

Third, ask Mary to help you. Why should we ask Mary to help when we've got Jesus? Recall that Jesus gave Mary to us from the Cross. The Church affirms it, and so does the Communion of Saints. One of Mary's titles is "Refuge of Sinners." The saints knew this, and she helped many become saints.

> The greater sinners we are, the more tenderness and compassion Mary has for us. The child who has cost the Mother the most tears is closest to her heart! (St. John Vianney, quoted in Charles G. Fehrenbach, *Mary Day by Day* [New York: Catholic Book Publishing, 1987], 89)

Mary is your mother. It took me a long time to get that; she is so patient! Just as we talked about father issues earlier, let's add mother issues to the list, along with the body issues that Mary can help us heal. Mary helps us move toward cherishing the women we were born to be.

Mary has no "body issues"! She is a *fully* redeemed woman, the New Eve. That means she has none of our hang-ups with the body and its sexuality. . . .

For those of us with "mother wounds," Mary's fully integrated motherhood is a glorious healing balm. . . . And she longs to share her loving-nurturing-spiritual-body-goodness with all of her children. She rejoices to carry us mystically in her womb, nurse us mystically at her breasts . . . cuddle us, sing to us. And whenever we stink up our lives with sin, she doesn't scold, she doesn't shame—she happily and readily changes our diapers, wiping our bottoms clean with her tender love and mercy (which is God's tender love and mercy). (Christopher West, *Heaven's Song: Sexual Love as It Was Meant to Be* [Philadelphia: Ascension Press, 2008], 80)

Even with three chapters on motherhood, we've just begun to explore the depths of maternity as God's good plan for women and for the world. But going forward from here, consider reaching for the hand of your spiritual mother, Mary. Ask her to walk with you daily.

What Mary has at the beginning, namely, sinlessness, all will have at the end of life if they cooperate with the gift of their embodiedness. Mary shows us to accept the gift of our embodiedness . . . the God-given sex of the body . . . the body is not an obstacle to be overcome but rather, a gift to be lived. Mary delights in her body, especially in . . . femininity. It is precisely in her gift of being a woman, that Mary was fashioned and called by God to be the *Theotokos* [Mother of God]. . . .

Just think what would have happened if Mary had rebelled against the gift of her feminine body! *We* would be in a very different situation today. (Calloway, *The Virgin Mary and Theology of the Body*, 55–56)

Here's a vision of hope for every woman stung by bad decisions and the pain of sin. It is the life of St. Mary Magdalene. First, imagine Mary Magdalene, one of the notorious sinners mentioned in the New Testament, from whom seven devils were cast out. When she met the God of love, she turned from her sins, converted, and lived to love and serve Jesus.

Now, here's a second picture to envision: At the foot of Jesus's Cross, the Gospel records that Mary Magdalene stood next to the Blessed Virgin Mary—the woman the Church declares the Mother of God and John Paul II called "the mirror and measure of femininity" (See *Angelus Message*, June 25, 1995, 3).

In the New Testament [Mary Magdalene] is mentioned among the women who accompanied Christ and ministered to Him (Lk 8:2–3), where it is also said that seven devils had been cast out of her (Mk 16:9). She is next named as standing at the foot of the cross (Mk 15:40; Mt 27:56; Jn 19:25; Lk 23:49). She saw Christ laid in the tomb, and she was the first recorded witness of the Resurrection. (Jn 20:11–18). (H. Pope, "St. Mary Magdalen," http://www.newadvent.org/cathen/09761a.htm, accessed on September 12, 2012)

If Mary Magdalene, with her checkered past, can stand with the Blessed Virgin Mary—the epitome of grace and womanhood—then we all have a chance to do the same. The Blessed Mother is truly the friend and refuge of sinners . . . a spiritual mother who loves and guides spiritual mothers-in-training. Thanks to Mary, and the saints who cheer us on, we can cherish the beauty of our womanhood!

Flowing from our celebrating and cherishing our femininity, the gift of womanhood is worthy of our protection. Our bodacious calling—our maternal mission—is our role in the new evangelization that the Church must take on. The time is now for women to shine their light and love as guardians of life.

Once again, echoing Elisabeth Leseur, our mission urges us to become the lark whose "perpetual song announces the dawn" in a darkened world. And, I would add, we do this in a thoroughly feminine way, in tune with our blessings and beauty.

We must be forces for good within a culture that has stopped cherishing the gifts of women in their fullness. We must work toward exemplifying a new feminism. Women's liberation, as I had understood it in the past, was incomplete. My core—my feminine genius—was often missing or criticized. Discovering my feminine genius opened my eyes to the real possibility of living a Christian feminism that values women in a beautiful totality, in harmony with their created design.

> It depends on women to promote a new feminism, one that rejects the imitation of men and one that seeks equality not from a position of power but rather from a position of love. . . . Not just a human love but more profoundly a divine love.
>
> This new feminism must be based on a deep reflection on the very nature and design of woman herself. (Doyle, *The Genius of Womanhood*, 85–86)

With Jesus and Mary for inspiration and grace, coupled with the timeless teachings of the Church, we can promote a Christian feminism that strives for equality, yet does not demean women or men or their gifts.

We must help build the culture from the inside out—by first being willing to be converted ourselves. By cherishing our blessedness and our beauty and by calling men to see the values we hold most dear, we will give birth to a profound complementarity that will encourage and inspire others. For many of us, we will need grace to build on nature; fortunately, grace is not in short supply. But this will be the challenge: In order to move into a new day, we will need to forgive the men we know for their past mistakes and mistreatments. And we need to forgive ourselves. When women see complementary and collaborative relationships with men as something worth working toward—rather than adding to continued irreverent domination coming from either side—we'll see changes for good.

Ultimately, men will protect and respect our femininity when we are willing to protect and respect our femininity.

The good of the Gospel is that it leads us to new life in Christ and, ultimately, eternal life in heaven. This gospel of life has a very practical application for Christians. A woman's influence in the world consists of being a guardian of life. We give witness to it in our very nature, and that should extend to the moral leadership we have wherever we live and work. A culture of life will rise or fall in direct proportion to its respect for womanhood.

John Paul II makes our mission clear, echoing and expanding the words of Paul VI:

> In transforming culture so that it supports life, women occupy a place, in thought and action, which is unique

and decisive. It depends on them to promote a "new feminism" which rejects the temptation of imitating models of "male domination," in order to acknowledge and affirm the true genius of women in every aspect of the life of society, and overcome all discrimination, violence and exploitation.

Making my own the words of the concluding message of the Second Vatican Council, I address to women this urgent appeal: "Reconcile people with life." You are called to bear witness to the meaning of genuine love, of that gift of self and of that acceptance of others which are present in a special way in the relationship of husband and wife, but which ought also to be at the heart of every other interpersonal relationship. The experience of motherhood makes you acutely aware of the other person and, at the same time, confers on you a particular task . . . [accepting] a person who is recognized and loved because of the dignity which comes from being a person and not from other considerations, such as usefulness, strength, intelligence, beauty or health. . . . It is the indispensable prerequisite for an authentic cultural change. (*Evangelium Vitae* [*On the Value and Inviolability of Human Life*], 99)

Life must stand bravely in the face of death. Like Mary, who stood at the foot of the Cross, we must see the Blessed Virgin Mary as the cornerstone of a new Christian feminism.

Each woman's life, well lived, might be the best gospel anyone will ever read. But before the doing, before the carrying out of the mission, there is the being. The personhood of each woman, without her ever saying a word or doing a thing, is a sign of life.

Womanhood and life.

These terms are inseparable.

Like Jesus and Mary.

Mary is the cornerstone of a new Christian feminism built upon Jesus, the cornerstone of Christianity.

In the new evangelization, Mary is the star, but Jesus is the sun.

What we've talked about in this book is a current running through a very deep ocean. I feel like a kid who waded into the water a little bit, then just skipped a smooth stone across the incoming waves of the beautiful azure sea. With each chapter, we've skimmed along, touching the surface at various points, but here is where the stone drops in and sinks, finishing its trajectory. There's so much more of the water beneath each ripple. Skipping rocks is only fun for so long. To be really refreshed, you've got to dive in.

I would love it if this book became a springboard for your diving more deeply. Use the resources listed in the back of this book to deepen your knowledge of prayer, scripture, theology of the body, the feminine genius and new feminism, the Catechism, and Mary. One excellent resource is Endow, a ministry dedicated to the Education on the Nature and Dignity of Women. Look for it in your diocese or online.

> It is thus my hope, dear sisters, that you will reflect carefully on what it means to speak of the *"genius of women,"* not only in order to be able to see in this phrase a specific part of God's plan which needs to be accepted and appreciated, but also in order to let this genius be more fully expressed in the life of society as a whole, as well as in the life of the Church. (John Paul II, *Letter to Women*, 10)

Conclusion to Part Three

If the things we've talked about in this book were new to you, let our conversations here be a prelude to the song God wants to sing through the rest of your life. If The Feminine Genius was a band playing a sold-out concert at Yankee Stadium, consider this book the warm-up band. Now that the opening act is over, remember that the real show is just getting started!

If you already knew much of what we've covered in these pages, I hope you were adding harmonies, tapping your feet to the tunes, and singing along with the familiar lyrics. I hope you will be the woman who shares her wealth of soul with the next gal, encouraging her to live "the life worthy of the calling to which you have been called" (Eph 4:1).

And so, we come to this final chorus.

O, bodacious woman! Sing!

Be the lark singing for all she is worth against the darkness in anticipation of the dawn!

You are *blessed*: with the immense dignity you have because of *who* you are and *whose* you are in your wonderful creation and holy Baptism.

You are *beautiful*: with the intrinsic qualities of your femininity (receptivity, generosity, sensitivity, and maternity)—gifts that are for you and that equip you, making your womanhood a true gift to others.

You are *bodacious*: with your most excellent and sacred mission of giving birth to light, love, and life!

Epilogue

A Mother, a Daughter, and a Pontiff

Before I skimmed the stone at the water's edge . . .

I was flying in a plane high in the air over the North Atlantic Ocean, at about 38,000 feet. I was in the zone, that creative place that enfolds you when you are working and where everything around you fades away as you concentrate. I was studying Pope John Paul II's 1995 Angelus messages focusing on the genius of women. As I read them, I was looking for an angle that would help me write about Catholic womanhood. I needed a theme, an organizing principle.

As I worked, I had many younger women on my mind, particularly one young woman. On that flight, I was winging my way to Paris for a mother-daughter reunion with my then-college-aged daughter who was studying abroad for the semester. It dawned on me how much I wished I had known some of these things about the gift of womanhood when I was her age. And yet, how blessed I was to have experienced so much of God's graces in spite of my lack of formal knowledge.

I kept reading, scribbling notes in the margins and whispering little prayers heavenward when something like a solitary lark appeared on the page in one of John Paul II's prayers in his *Angelus Address*:

> May the Blessed Virgin help men and women in our time
> clearly understand God's plan for femininity.
> Called to the highest vocation of divine motherhood,
> Our Lady is the exemplary woman. . . .

165

May Mary obtain for women throughout the world
an enlightened and active awareness
of their dignity, gifts, and mission.
(June 18, 1995, 3)

And I began to sing.

Acknowledgments

Many thanks to the women in the Catholic parishes that I've belonged to and served in, both in Massachusetts and New York. Special mention goes to the Mothers' Morning of Prayer and the women of FIRE, who exemplified spiritual motherhood in my life.

To Dr. Maura Hearden, assistant professor of theology at DeSales University, my gratitude for your thoughtful, timely help and support.

Bodacious thanks belongs to author Lisa Hendey, founder of *CatholicMom.com*, for your receptivity of my work, your generosity in friendship, and your invitation to give podcasting a try.

Deep appreciation belongs to the *Among Women* podcast listeners and readers of my blog, Facebook page, and Twitter feed. Thank you also to the media apostolate of SQPN for its support of *Among Women* and the new evangelization.

To all the editors I've worked for over the years, especially those who labor to feature Catholic content online and in print, thank you for the guidance, the camaraderie, and especially, the work. Here's a hat tip to the nurturing community of the Catholic Writers Guild.

My heartfelt thanks to everyone who said a prayer for this book, was a friendly reader of the manuscript, or had a conversation with me about its themes.

Humble thanks to the entire Ave Maria Press team, especially associate editor Kristi McDonald for her early enthusiasm and subsequent care of this project, and deep gratitude to editorial director Bob Hamma and publisher Tom Grady.

To Terry Polakovic: thanks for blessing me with your forword and for serving Catholic women throughout North America through the ministry of Endow.

In memoriam: Judit Komaromi (1950–2006), who showed me the face of hope and told me to keep writing.

Muchas gracias mi amiga, María Morera Johnson, English faculty member at Georgia Piedmont Technical College, for your editorial prowess, kind consideration of innumerable drafts, and ability to raise the writing fun quotient in the process.

Thanks, most especially, to my sisters, Peg Oliveira and Pam Kehoe, for your good humor and holy influence. And to my mom and dad, Cathy and Jim Wilhelm, who nicknamed us girls "the Three Ps," loving thanks for the sacrifices that sent us to Catholic schools, where I first learned to love writing.

I offer thanks to God for the gifts of my now-grown children, Bobby, Katie, and Peter. I count being your mother among my deepest joys.

Finally, to my husband, Bob, for whom a thank you doesn't even begin to cover it. Your faith-filled optimism has inspired me since we met. Thanks for sending me back to graduate school and believing that a theology degree had merit and promise. Your love and fidelity, after more than thirty years together, still makes my heart sing.

Suggested Readings and Resources

These readings and resources are listed by chapter, with additional listings at the end.

Foreword

Endow is a ministry of the Catholic Church, established in the Archdiocese of Denver and active in several dioceses in the United States and Canada. Endow brings women together to discover their God-given dignity and to understand their role in humanizing and transforming society. Endow utilizes small study groups, conferences, and retreats to cultivate faith, fellowship, and formation. For details: http://endowgroups.org.

Introduction

Go to PatGohn.com to find links to my columns, speaking dates, the *Among Women* podcast, and more.

Chapter 1 : Living from the Inside Out

When looking up Bible references, try to read more than just the verses cited. If possible, read the whole chapter where the verses are found in order to understand the context. For example, in this chapter, the quotations from Luke's gospel referencing Mary's ponderings (Lk 1:29, 2:19, 51) are part of a larger section about the annunciation, visitation, and Nativity.

See paragraphs 14–16 of the 1965 Vatican II document *Gaudium et Spes* (The Pastoral Constitution on the Church in the Modern World) to find a discussion of body and soul and conscience. You can access this document online at www.vatican. va/archive/hist_councils/ii_vatican_council/documents/ vat-ii_cons_19651207_gaudium-et-spes_en.html.

If you want to familiarize yourself with the major themes of Vatican II, start by reading *Lumen Gentium* (The Dogmatic Constitution on the Church). *Gaudium et Spes*, *Lumen Gentium*, and all sixteen documents of Vatican II can be found in print through a

Catholic bookstore or online at the Vatican website: www.vatican.
va/archive/hist_councils/ii_vatican_council/index.htm.

Chapter 2: God's Good Opinion of You

You may wish to read all of Psalm 139, and I recommend that
you read the first three chapters of the book of Genesis, as back-
ground to this chapter.

Chapter 3: Your Soul's Tattoo

The *Catechism of the Catholic Church* is a valuable reference tool.
Find a print copy through your Catholic bookseller, or access it
online at the Vatican website: www.vatican.va/archive/ccc/index.
htm. Or, find a useful, searchable online catechism here: http://
www.scborromeo.org/ccc.htm. (Note: the catechism, or CCC, is
referenced by paragraph numbers, not page numbers.)

To read about the Blessed Trinity in the catechism, turn to CCC
221, 232, 237, 249, 253–56, 260–67.

Mary Healy, *Men and Women Are from Eden: A Study Guide to
John Paul II's Theology of the Body* (Cincinnati: Servant, 2005). This
book is a concise summary with a study guide on John Paul II's
theology of the body.

Mulieris Dignitatem (On the Dignity and Vocation of Women)
is from John Paul II. It is available online: www.vatican.va/
holy_father/john_paul_ii /apost_letters/documents/hf_jp-ii_
apl_15081988_mulieris-dignitatem_en.html. This is a document we
return to again and again in this book. This is important reading
for women.

T. S. Eliot, *The Four Quartets* (New York: Harcourt and Brace,
1943). I've added this reference for the poetry fans out there. Also
available online at http://en.wikiquote.org/wiki/Four_Quartets.

Check the catechism to read "On God the Father" (CCC, 232,
239–48) and "On the Lord's Prayer" (CCC, 2759–865). The latter
offers excellent line-by-line teaching on that prayer. Also, read about
Baptism at CCC, 977, 1213–84.

Read John 10:1–30 for more teaching on the Good Shepherd and
Jesus identifying himself as being one with the Father.

Redemptoris Mater (Mother of the Redeemer, On the Blessed Virgin Mary in the Life of the Pilgrim Church, 1987). This is John Paul II's major encyclical on Mary. It can be found online at www. vatican.va/holy_father/john_paul_ii /encyclicals/documents/ hf_jp-ii_enc_25031987_redemptoris-mater_en.html.

St. Louis de Montfort is quoted at the end of the chapter. His book *True Devotion to Mary* is considered a spiritual classic on Mary and Marian devotion, and it is said to have had a profound influence on John Paul II. A recent edition was published by TAN Books in 2007.

Chapter 4: Saying Yes to Love

John 15:9–16 is quoted in the chapter. Jesus' words are set in the larger context of his final discourse, or his words and prayers to the apostles at the Last Supper. The entire discourse spans four chapters, John 13:31–16:33.

This would also be a good time to read (or reread Luke 1) while considering Mary's *fiat*.

The many General Audiences of John Paul II's catechesis on theology of the body are best read in English in *Man and Woman He Created Them: A Theology of the Body*, by John Paul II, trans. Michael Waldstein (Boston: Pauline Books & Media, 2006.) This is a comprehensive academic resource on the subject.

John Paul II's *Letter to Women* is an important document. Like *Mulieris Dignitatem*, this letter is a must-read. Find it online at www.vatican.va/holy_father/john_paul_ii/letters/documents/ hf_jp-ii_let_29061995_women_en.html.

Chapter 5: Making a Gift of Yourself

A major theme found in theology of the body is taken from *Gaudium et Spes*. "Making a sincere gift of oneself" is found in par. 24 §3.

The Sound of Music, a five-time Oscar-winning film, was made in 1965. Rated G.

Read Luke 1:39–56. Mary's *Magnificat* is set within the context of the visitation with Elizabeth.

Chapter 6: Seeing with Your Heart

St. Teresa Benedicta of the Cross, *Essays on Women (The Collected Works of Edith Stein)*, trans. Freda Mary Oben (Washington, DC: ICS, 1996). The book is a collection of some of Edith Stein's academic writings. She was canonized after being martyred during World War II.

Mary Jo Anderson, "Feminine Genius," *Catholic Answers* [formerly This Rock Magazine], July/August 2005, 18-21, http://www.catholicculture.org/culture/library/view.cfm?recnum=6709.

Elisabeth Leseur, *Selected Writings* (Mahwah, NJ: Paulist Press, 2005). These letters and essays are from a very devout wife and mother from the early twentieth century. Her cause for canonization has been under way for years.

Mary Poplin, *Finding Calcutta: What Mother Teresa Taught Me About Meaningful Work and Service* (Downers Grove, IL: InterVarsity Press, 2008). There are many books about the life and values of Mother Teresa of Calcutta; this one introduced me to the words of Mother Teresa that were quoted in the chapter.

Chapter 7: Entrusting Your Maternity to Eternity

Donald H. Calloway, M.I.C., *The Virgin Mary and Theology of the Body* (West Chester, PA: Marian Press, 2005). The book contains a series of academic theological essays on Mary and theology of the body.

Ecclesia de Eucharistia is (2003) is the final encyclical penned by John Paul II, and it focuses on the Eucharist and its relationship to the Church.

Chapter 8: Raising Saints for Heaven

Alice von Hildebrand, *The Privilege of Being a Woman*, 6th ed. (Naples, FL: Sapientia Press, 2007). This is a short, scholarly, yet very readable volume.

Lumen Gentium deals with "the domestic church" of the home, and much more. It is an excellent document to read in its entirely and is often called the key that unlocks the themes of Vatican II. If you have time to read only one document about the Church, this is it.

Cardinal Joseph Mindszenty's ode to motherhood can be purchased on a gift card at http://www.mindszenty.org/Mother_father.aspx.

Fulton J. Sheen, *The World's First Love: Mary, Mother of God* (San Francisco: Ignatius Press, 1996) is a soon-to-be spiritual classic from this twentieth-century Catholic televangelist, as Sheen's cause of canonization is under way. It is lovingly written for a mother.

Stefano Manelli, O.F.M., *Jesus Our Eucharistic Love* (1973). The book can be found online at http://www.marys-touch.com/Eucharist/ch6.htm.

Chapter 9: Beyond Fairy Godmothers

Katrina J. Zeno, *Discovering the Feminine Genius: Every Woman's Journey* (Boston: Pauline Books & Media, 2010). This is a republishing of an earlier book. It's very energetic and easily digested.

Karen Doyle, *The Genius of Womanhood* (Boston: Pauline Books & Media, 2009). The book is a short, inspirational keepsake book on the themes of womanhood.

St. Thérèse of Lisieux, *The Story of a Soul: The Autobiography of Saint Thérèse of Lisieux*, trans. John Clarke, O.C.D., 3rd ed. (Washington, DC: ICS Publications, 1996. It is also available online at ·http://www.gutenberg.org/cache/epub/16772/pg16772.txt. This is a spiritual classic that describes the saint's life and her spirituality, also known as the "little way."

Eucharistic Adoration for the Sanctification of Priests and Spiritual Motherhood, Congregation for the Clergy. This document recommends praying for priests as an important part of spiritual maternity. It can be read online at http://www.clerus.org/clerus/dati/2008-01/25-13/Adoration.pdf.

Benedict XVI, *Homily*, August 15, 2005. Pope Benedict has done much scholarly writing on Mary, yet this homily is from the heart. Find it here: www.vatican.va/holy_father/benedict_xvi /homilies/2005/documents/hf_ben-xvi_hom_20050815_assunzione-maria_en.html.

Chapter 10: Our Bodacious Calling

Charles Fehrenbach, *Mary Day by Day* (New York: Catholic Book Publishing, 1987). This keepsake book is a pocket-sized prayer book filled with scripture, short quotations from saints and popes, and prayers for Marian devotion.

Christopher West, *Heaven's Song: Sexual Love as It Was Meant to Be* (West Chester, PA: Ascension Press, 2008). West is one of the leading teacher-evangelists for theology of the body. This is a great book, but perhaps it's not the book to start with if you are first learning about theology of the body. See other resources from West listed in the list of additional recommendations below.

In this chapter, you'll find the *Catholic Encyclopedia* quoting scripture references about Mary Magdalene. New Advent is a website that has a search engine for the Catholic Encyclopedia, as well as a front page with news and articles. Find it here: www. newadvent.org/.

Kieran Kavanaugh and Otilio Rodriguez, trans., *The Collected Works of St. John of the Cross* (Washington, DC: ICS Publications, 1991). St. John of the Cross is one of the great spiritual directors from the Middle Ages.

This chapter briefly references St. Francis de Sales, whose quote comes from this book: *Francis De Sales, Jane De Chantal: Letters of Spiritual Direction* (Mahwah, NJ: Paulist Press, 1988). His most famous book is Introduction to the Devout Life, and I highly recommend it.

Additional Recommendations

Books

Helen Alvaré, editor, *Breaking Through: Catholic Women Speak for Themselves* (Huntington, IN: Our Sunday Visitor, 2012). A powerful collection of essays on the integration of faith and life when it comes to politics, popular culture, and women's issues.

Andrew Apostoli, *Walk Humbly With Your God: Simple Steps to a Virtuous Life* (Cincinnati: Servant, 2006). If you need help developing or maintaining a Christian life that includes advice on how to pray, this book is excellent.

Erika Bachiochi, *Women, Sex, and the Church* (Boston: Pauline Books & Media, 2010). Intelligent and frank, here you'll find some of the best essays on the subjects of new feminism, love, sex, reproduction, contraception, abortion, ordination, and more.

Sr Helena Burns F.S.P., *He Speaks to You*, (Boston: Pauline Books & Media, 2012). This is a book to pray with. It will also help you discern your vocation as a woman. Tailored for young women in search of God's will for their life, it's a gift for any woman who would like daily prayer, inspiration, and encouragement.

Brian Butler and Jason and Crystalina Evert, *Theology of the Body for Teens* (West Chester, PA: Ascension Press, 2006). An introductory course for teens. Find it here: http://thetheologyofthebody.com/book-resources /study-information/1825/ tob-teens-high-school-edition-about.

Colleen Carroll Campbell, *My Sisters the Saints: A Spiritual Memoir* (New York: Image Books, 2012). This well-told memoir from Campbell, a journalist, and former White House speechwriter, describes her quest for meaning in light of her Catholic faith and contemporary feminism. Her story is woven with wisdom from St. Teresa of Avila, St. Faustina Kowalska, St. Teresa Benedicta of the Cross, St. Thérèse of Lisieux, Blessed Teresa of Calcutta, and the Blessed Virgin Mary.

Francis Coomes, S.J., *Mother's Manual* (Brooklyn, New York: William J. Hirten, 2000). This is the little book held my prayer together during my pregnancies.

Mary Eberstadt, *Adam and Eve after the Pill: Paradoxes of the Sexual Revolution* (San Francisco: Ignatius Press, 2012). This has excellent social, religious, and political commentary on its subject matter.

Dawn Eden, *My Peace I Give You: Healing Sexual Wounds with the Help of the Saints* (Notre Dame, IN: Ave Maria Press, 2012). This book shares the author's journey of healing from childhood abuse and offers numerous insights for recovery, healing, and ongoing conversion.

Michael Gaitley, M.I.C., *33 Days to Morning Glory: A Do-It-Yourself Retreat in Preparation for Marian Consecration* (Stockbridge, MA: Marian Press, 2011). This book contains insightful teachings about Marian devotion and prayers from St. Louis de Montfort, St.

Maximilian Kolbe, Mother Teresa of Calcutta, and John Paul II. A consecration to Jesus through Mary is a prayer to live every day as a daughter or son of Mary.

A Scriptural Rosary (Glenview, IL: Christianica Center, 1961). I've used this pocket-sized prayer book for over twenty-five years. No experience is necessary when it comes to learning to pray the Rosary. The scriptural content explains the Mysteries of the Rosary, allowing readers to meditate on the significant events in the lives of Jesus and Mary.

Lisa M. Hendey, *The Handbook for Catholic Moms: Nurturing Your Heart, Mind, Body, and Soul* (Notre Dame, IN: Ave Maria Press, 2010). Here you'll find helpful prayers, encouragement, and perspective for mothers with children. The author is also the founder of CatholicMom.com, a great online resource for parents and families. Hendey's second book is a great follow-up to the first: *A Book of Saints for Catholic Moms* (Notre Dame, IN: Ave Maria Press, 2011).

Hallie Lord, *Style, Sex, and Substance: 10 Catholic Women Consider the Things that Really Matter* (Cincinnati: Servant, 2012). This book is a series of essays from popular Catholic authors and bloggers.

Mark Miravalle, *Introduction to Mary: The Heart of Marian Doctrine and Devotion* (Goleta, CA: Queenship Publishing, 1997). If you have questions about Mary or Marian doctrine, this is a great reference book.

Janet Smith, ed., *Why Humanae Vitae Was Right: A Reader* (San Francisco: Ignatius Press, 1993). Smith has gathered outstanding essays to demonstrate why contraception is a moral evil and its use is not compatible with human dignity, sexual responsibility, and spousal love.

Emily Stimpson, *The Catholic Girl's Survival Guide for the Single Years: The Nuts and Bolts of Staying Sane and Happy While Waiting for Mr. Right* (Steubenville, OH: Emmaus Road Publishing, 2012). This book is for women in their twenties and thirties who discern a call to marriage but are wondering what to do until then.

Teresa Tomeo, *Exteme Makeover: Women Transformed by Christ, Not by the Culture* (San Francisco: Ignatius Press, 2011) Former TV news journalist turned Catholic evangelist on EWTN radio and television, Tomeo takes on the latest research on social behavior and culture trends. She builds a case that it is not the sexual revolution that frees and dignifies women, but the teachings of the Catholic Church.

Christopher West, *At the Heart of the Gospel: Reclaiming the Body for the New Evangelization* (New York: Image Books, 2012). West's book deals with the theology of the body as it intersects the new evangelization.

Christopher West, *Theology of the Body for Beginners* (West Chester, PA: Ascension Press, 2004). This short beginner's book is an easy-to-read executive summary.

Christopher West, *Theology of the Body Explained* (Boston: Pauline Books & Media, 2003). This book contains much more in-depth analysis, heavily footnoted with quotations from the writings of John Paul II.

Kate Wicker, *Weightless: Making Peace with Your Body* (Cincinnati: Servant, 2011). This is a helpful book for dealing with body issues or eating disorders.

Resources

Among Women: a podcast celebrating the beauty and grace of Catholic faith and life from a woman's perspective, with Pat Gohn. Find it at www.amongwomenpodcast.com or via PatGohn.com.

Busted Halo: an online ministry that strives to reveal the spiritual dimension of our lives through feature stories, reviews, interviews, faith guides, commentaries, audio clips, discussions and connections to retreat, worship, and service opportunities. See http://bustedhalo.com.

Magnificat: a daily devotional to help you grow in your spiritual life, with daily prayers, Mass readings, articles, and inspiration. Subscribe here: https://www.magnificat.net/english/index.asp.

The Mary Page: Maintained by the Marian Library at University of Dayton, this site contains very reliable information about Blessed Virgin Mary. Go to http://campus.udayton.edu/mary.

Rachel's Vineyard: retreats and counseling to help you and your family find healing from the pain of abortion. Go to www.rachels-vineyard.org.

Project Rachel: more hope after abortion. Visit http://hopeafterabortion.com.

SQPN: a new media apostolate featuring podcasts offering Catholic content that is both entertaining and informative. Go to http://sqpn.com.

Theology of the Body International Alliance: learn more about theology of the body through this valuable resource. Find it at http://www.theologyofthebody.net.

The Vatican website offers news and information about Catholicism, plus homilies, speeches, and documents the popes write, and more. Check out http://www.vatican.va/phome_en.htm.

Word on Fire: learn about the Catholic faith with books, podcasts, articles, videos, and more, including the film series *Catholicism*. See http://www.wordonfire.org.

Women of Grace: Check the website for an assortment of books and programming available at http://www.womenofgrace.com.

Pat Gohn is a popular Catholic writer, speaker, and host of the *Among Women* podcast, affiliated with the Star Quest Production Network (SQPN). At the forefront of Catholic media, Gohn writes regular columns at *Patheos, CatholicMom. com,* and *Amazing Catechists,* and has contributed to *Catholic Digest, Catholic Exchange,* and many other sites. Gohn's areas of expertise are faith formation and women's ministry. She holds a master's degree in theology and Christian ministry from Franciscan University of Steubenville, plus certificates in adult faith formation leadership and theology of the body from the University of Dayton and the Theology of the Body Institute respectively. She has led parish-based ministries for more than thirty years, including service in the largest parish in the Archdiocese of Boston.

Gohn's media company, Behold Communications, produces Catholic content for catechetical publications, commercial and non-profit clients, and voice-overs for radio, Internet, and audio books. Gohn and her husband live in Massachusetts and have three grown children.

AVE

AVE MARIA PRESS

Founded in 1865, Ave Maria Press,
a ministry of the Congregation of
Holy Cross, is a Catholic publishing
company that serves the spiritual and
formative needs of the Church and its
schools, institutions, and ministers;
Christian individuals and families; and
others seeking spiritual nourishment.

For a complete listing of titles from

Ave Maria Press

Sorin Books

Forest of Peace

Christian Classics

visit www.avemariapress.com

AVE MARIA PRESS
Notre Dame, IN
A Ministry of the United States Province of Holy Cross